A GOOD
DAY'S
WORK

ALSO BY JOHN DEMONT

Citizens Irving: K.C.Irving and His Legacy

Coal Black Heart: The Story of Coal and Lives it Ruled

The Last Best Place: Lost in the Heart of Nova Scotia

A GOOD DAY'S WORK

IN PURSUIT *of a* DISAPPEARING CANADA

JOHN DeMONT

DOUBLEDAY CANADA

Doubleday Canada and colophon are registered trademarks

LIBRARY AND ARCHIVES CANADA CATALOGUING IN PUBLICATION

DeMont, John, 1956-, author

A good day's work : in pursuit of a disappearing Canada / John DeMont.

Includes index.

Issued in print and electronic formats.

ISBN 978-0-385-66506-3

1. Labor—Canada—History. 2. Professions—Canada—History. I. Title.

HD8104.D46 2013   331.0971   C2013-902639-8

Cover and text design: Five Seventeen
Cover image: History Collection, Nova Scotia Museum

IMAGE CREDITS
Page v courtesy of author
Pages 19, 47, 73, 97, 123, 155, 179, 205 and 231 © Shutterstock.com/ Everett
Collection; Pages 21, 75, 99, 125, 207, 233 and 257 © Shutterstock.com/
RetroClipArt; Page 49 © Shutterstock.com/ Aleksei Makarov; Page 157 ©
Shutterstock.com/ Leyn; Page 181 © Shutterstock.com/ Makar; Page 255 ©
Shutterstock.com/ Rook76; photo frames © Shutterstock.com/ Vilaly Korovin.

Printed and bound in the USA

Published in Canada by Doubleday Canada,
a division of Random House of Canada Limited

www.randomhouse.ca

10 9 8 7 6 5 4 3 2 1

To Lisa Napier

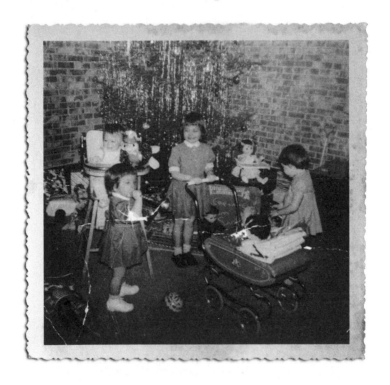

CONTENTS

PROLOGUE

I LIVE in the city where I was born. This is, mostly, a happy state of affairs. I've moved around, but Halifax is a good place to be because of what it is—easy on the eye, a little crazy, naturally laid-back without being drearily tranquil—and what it was. A kind of personal archaeology is possible here. Those possessing a certain frame of mind can glimpse the ruins of the past amid the structures of the present. I'm not talking about the stuff that tourists, guidebooks in hand, seek: the mouldering buildings, the scenes of ancient bloodletting, the unassuming corners where this guy and that started before going on to great things. Halifax, by Canadian standards, is an old place. There's a ton of that kind of history around for those who want it. It's just not what I need.

What I need when my forebrain bulges, and the dog knows enough to give me a wide berth, is to tread the landscape I walked when I was young. I realize I'm not alone in this. My research—well, I asked a few people—has shown me that the yen surely seems to grow as time passes. It's not surprising. The day will come when the fog of dementia descends on your elders and people your age start to take their leave. Eventually university kids hold open doors and call you "sir." And your hamstrings become so tight that only by laying turtled on your back can you pull put your socks on . . . at this point I think it's perfectly natural to want to breathe the air you breathed when life was all out there, waiting for you.

I'm lucky because I just have to walk out the door. Then I'm immediately on terrain where every house, street, building, patch of playground grass or chunk of schoolyard concrete, on the right day can summon up the pang of memory. From the ages of six to nine I lived in a small, slant-roofed, white wooden house with my parents and younger brother about three minutes east of where I now live. Sometime in 1965 we packed up and made the eight-block drive in a fin-backed Buick to where the street was a little wider and the lots a little bigger. For the rest of my school years that is where we lived: in another white wooden house in a neighbourhood where everything mind-blowing I remember about childhood happened.

The house at 1681 Cambridge Street is a khaki colour now and, of course, smaller than it seemed at the time. When I stroll by alone, as I sometimes do, it's like I'm some kind of ghost looking into the second-floor window where my bedroom used to be. In my mind I see my dad standing in the den, simultaneously watching *The Wild Wild West* on the black-and-white

TV and continuing a lifelong quest to groove his golf swing. Out in the kitchen, past the living room where no one sat and the dining room where people seldom ate, I picture my mom, slim of figure, hair in a Donna Reed pageboy, putting away the supper dishes and taking the occasional pull on a Player's Mild smouldering in an ashtray. Then my memory takes me out the back door to the then-unpaved lane that ran behind our house. I see a crewcut kid and my little brother, hear the smack of the horsehide baseball landing in the Rawlings leather gloves and smell the salty evening air.

In my mind it is 1967, because that's probably as good a reference point as any. Do you remember '67? When, at a hundred, Canada seemed to be suspended midway between the old and the new? The year of Expo, Man and His World. A time when Canada's economy was shooting on all cylinders and we as a country were as prosperous as we'd ever be. This place, even an eleven-year-old could see, was coming of age. We had our own flag. A hockey team in Toronto—back in the Precambrian days when only six NHL franchises existed—was on its way to winning its last Stanley Cup.

I know, I know: revolution was in the air. The streets of America were aflame. Che was dead. Israeli tanks rumbled into Gaza Strip. In Canada, Quebecers were jazzed by the notion of independence and the young luxuriated in the pot-befogged coffee houses of Toronto's Yorkville. But Pierre Berton labelled 1967 Canada's "Last Good Year" for a reason. The truth was that in 1967, if it was great to be alive, then to be a young boy living in a comfortable house on a pleasant street in Halifax made you want to get up and do the Mashed Potato.

SOMETIMES I take out a black-and-white picture of James Grant's 1967 grade six class at Sir Charles Tupper School. We did not look like people about to set the world ablaze. With a few exceptions—a pair of Jewish brothers, two girls with French-speaking parents and one young woman with an English accent—we were startlingly uniform: the pasty-faced descendants of Celts and Brits, as befitting a province settled mainly by English, Irish and Scots. This is how hick a town we were: an Australian-born kid landed in our midst a year or so later. We nicknamed him "Skippy the Bush Kangaroo" after a show we watched on television.

Looking at that school picture, I find it hard to imagine him really caring. We wore glasses with Coke-bottle lenses that magnified the eyes like Jerry Lewis's in *The Nutty Professor*. This was before orthodontists owned islands in the South Pacific, so most of us, I'm guessing, had teeth like dragons. Some of the girls would later in life join wacko religious cults and pair up with bad men. Yet radical fervor did not seem to simmer among these wearers of pleated skirts, knee socks, penny loafers and regulation navy blue jumpers. Or for that matter among the boys, all of us yearning to be as flinty-eyed as Linc Hayes in *The Mod Squad*, as spectacularly as that ideal contrasted with the sports jackets, ties and cardigans—the bowl cuts and wet-down-with-spit side parts—that live forever in that class photo.

We were, largely, Sunday-school students. We Sang "O Canada" at the start of every school day and, in many cases, still said the Lord's Prayer before we hit the hay at night. Somewhere nuclear missiles sat in silos ready to exterminate entire generations. But in these innocent times my buddies and I mostly wanted to debate the merits of Mary Ann on *Gilligan's Island* versus those of the daughter with the go-go boots on *Lost in Space*.

Bobby Orr and Napoleon Solo were our transcendent heroes. Since we had yet to discover Dad's *Playboy* stash, the only printed material most of us came in contact with outside the classroom was the pile of *Dr. Strange, The Ghost Rider* and *Rawhide Kid* comics under our bed. Halifax, in those days, had a pair of television stations, three radio stations and morning and afternoon newspapers. We might as well have been ancient Mesopotamians scanning the skies in search of signs of enlightenment from the gods, because the sum total of what we knew was nothing.

If any of the dads were hitting the Canadian Club or the wife, none of us knew it. If any of the moms got wrecked on tranqs and ran off with a hairdresser, well, that was news to us. Big sisters undoubtedly had abortions; older brothers were getting their first taste of blotter acid. All this would have come as revelation too.

Where we lived I thought of as central Halifax or "Quinpool," after the main drag; or "over by Dal," a reference to Dalhousie University. But some people thought of it as the edge of "the South End," where the city's most comfortable burghers lived. Our parents were members of the Imperial Order of the Daughters of the Empire and the Benevolent and Protective Order of the Elks of Canada. They paid their taxes. They voted in Bob Stanfield, a stolid long-johns magnate, as premier for four straight terms. We were the offspring of small-business owners, bank managers, accountants, teachers and university professors. The daughter of the owner of both of the city's newspapers was a classmate. So was a young woman whose dad would later become president of Dalhousie. A couple of classmates were, I guess, genuinely wealthy by the standards of a Maritime Canadian city in the sixties. But the only way we might have understood their privilege was when they got new hockey gear every Christmas or could afford a Mountain Dew to go with the popcorn in the box with the scary clown face for the Saturday matinee at the Oxford Theatre.

Our city, with a population of just 93,000, was small. But we didn't comprehend that either. Nor did we know that Halifax, a port town, was once considered the wickedest town in North America. During the war years, it was still a place of whorehouses and opium dens, a town that exploded in an orgy of drinking, looting and public fornication when peace was declared on VE day. In 1967 hookers strolled in front of the Lieutenant-Governor's residence and Hells Angels were muscling into the drug trade. Of the 134 listings under restaurants and taverns in the 1967 city directory, only seventeen had lounge, bar or tavern in the name. But libations, I later learned, could be had at Billy Downey's Arrow's Club, where great soul and R and B bands performed, or at the Resolute Club, habituated by the city's expat Newfoundlanders, or the Surf Club on Barrington Street, home to navy men. I never knew what exactly was served up at the Prize Fighter's Club on Creighton Street. But a double rum and Coke was forever available at the Greco-Canadian Social Club, an establishment with which I would one day become well acquainted.

That, though, came far later. For kids careening toward teen age in 1967, this place, where men still wore hats and every crossing guard was named Al, was a whole world of bygone glories in a few city blocks. All you needed was a bicycle with a banana seat, and a Sandy Koufax card clipped with a clothespin to the spokes of the rear wheel so that the bike sounded like it was motorized. Or just a pair of Adidas sneakers, the white ones with the blue stripes, You could pump up leafy Jubilee Road, past Murray's, where moms sent their progeny for smokes, and Payne's with the glass showcase manned by a real-life butcher in a white apron and hat. You might veer down Edward Street, past the little stone post office, then cut up Coburg Road, where for a dime and a used Fanta Orange bottle you could pull the latest *Sgt. Fury and His Howling Commandos* from a wire rack inside a drugstore that had relocated from the city's downtown after the VE-day riots. You might take a detour through a cemetery where Confederate soldiers, Norwegian, Dutch and British sailors from the Second World War, a few Fathers of Confederation and an industrialist or two are buried. Then you might fly steeply downhill to the Horse Field, the playground on the edge of the railway cut, where in a year or so my compadres and I could be glimpsed sitting in the branches of a big tree, smoking wine-tipped cigarillos. If you went far enough, you could strip off T-shirt and shorts and dive into the waters of the Halifax Arm, back in the innocent days when people still did such things.

Whichever way you went you passed places of worship because the spirit mattered in this small city, which at that point boasted ten Anglican churches, as well as seven for Baptists, three for members of the Salvation Army, two synagogues—both in my neighbourhood—and a smattering of worship homes for Christian Scientists, Jehovah's Witnesses,

Pentecostals and the Greek Orthodox. The city had eleven United churches, including St. Andrew's, which the DeMonts regularly attended. Adherents of the Roman Catholic faith, in 1967, could choose from ten churches for Sunday mass. The closest was blocky, stone St. Thomas Aquinas, not a hundred yards from our house. But at that point, the Catholics in the area had their own nun-taught school system, which meant that other than the occasional bout of after-school sectarian violence, we didn't mix much with the Catholic kids.

All paths, sooner or later, seemed to lead to Quinpool Road, which carried traffic from the fishing villages and bedroom communities back and forth to the downtown. There we bought Black Cat bubble gum at the Candy Bowl and caps for our six-shooters at the 5¢ to $1 Store. At the Bluenose Hobby Shop we stared reverently at Aurora model kits of Godzilla and a Japanese Zero. Inside establishments with candy-striped barber poles at the entrance, we'd climb into chairs you could adjust up and down. Their owners, overjoyed to see that not everyone was letting their hair hang down, would unfurl white aprons, tie the ends around our chicken necks and ask our moms, "How short?" We usually went to Saturday matinees at the Oxford, one of Halifax's eight movie theatres, and sometimes, for birthday parties, headed for the Hyland on the street's westernmost end. In a couple of years, when we were old enough for paper routes, we would gather after delivering the *Chronicle Herald* on Saturday mornings for pancakes at the Ardmore Tea Room. But at age eleven a few of us already knew enough to make our way past the Blossom Shop, Leverman Credit Union, Reliable TV, Quinpool Shoe Repair and Dorothy Richards Corset Specialty Shop to the

Maritime Campus Store in the hope of glimpsing an honest-to-goodness co-ed.

Everything came together in the wondrous year of 1967. Jim Grant was definitely one of the best teachers I ever had. One of our crew—may the gods to this day still reward him—convinced the Miller sisters to play tackle football with us. We won our Little League baseball championship when the best athlete I had ever seen—a guy who would only live another six years before hanging himself in a vacant lot—drilled a ground ball toward third base at the same time as I put my glove in front of my face in self-defence.

Sometimes I think about how little has changed since that glorious summer of '67 when a guy named Irwin nearly left me in a vegetative state. Mostly, though, I think that forty-five years is a very long time. And I find myself increasingly driven to explain to everyone who will listen what Halifax used to be like.

⌒

THIS did not happen overnight. There was no single moment when I ceased looking hopefully forward and began peering mournfully back. I did not stop mid-sentence one day and slap my forehead in the realization that I had become one of those old coots who believes that the past is the only place where anything monumental occurs. Nor do I see myself as one of those reactionary tools longing for the good old days before same-sex marriage and turbans in the RCMP, when blacks, Jews, Indians and girls knew their place. I acknowledge that this neighbourhood where I live, this city—heck, the entire country—is getting better, every day, in so many ways. In the twenty-first century of this global world, change is a necessity along with a virtue. That doesn't stop a person from thinking about how things used to be.

I just have to look out the window, at the elementary school next door. Each noon hour a few dozen parents show up to escort their kids the few blocks home through the mean streets of residential Halifax, where, I guess, gangbangers and pedophiles roam. I went to the school that carried the same name nearly half a century ago: I can remember precisely one child whose parents showed up to walk her home: the dad wore a hat, suit, tie and overcoat in the hottest weather; the mom had the whiff of religious fundamentalism.

The schoolyard where we used to throw the football, skate and play Red Rover until it got too dark to see is now vacant minutes after the bell rings. Halifax kids, you see, don't wander free and mess around in schoolyards and vacant construction sites the way we used to. They're in daycare now, on parent-organized play dates or enrolled in swanky after-school programs to learn Irish dance and tae kwon do .

That's a little sad. It is also what people today call a "First World problem." Except sometimes I actually get out of my neighbourhood and drive through the close-knit towns my parents grew up in. To hear them tell it, home was a place where the smells of comfort food floated from open windows, lovable oddballs roamed the streets and everyone looked after everyone else. Now, with their mines and steel mills gone, those towns are harder places in which the young no longer stick around. All over this country, it seems, the dream of a sweet life in a small town is dying; rural areas are hollowing out. Most Canadians now huddle in cities along the Trans-Canada Highway, where they live in houses surrounded by hedges or gates in suburbs where farmland once rolled. Roots can be shallow in communities without sidewalks or central gathering places, where everyone must get behind the wheel of a car to take the kids to school or buy groceries. Neighbours don't necessarily watch each other's backs at a time and in a place when we're more likely than ever before to let others fall by the wayside.

I know what you're asking: What about the shining example of a modern-day multinational melting pot that Canada sets for the world? What about our tolerance? What about our modesty, sense of proportion and inherent fairness? I don't dispute any of that for a second. Except I still feel the urge to tell my kids that as good as things are, once it was different in this country. I want to tell them that there was a time when our hockey teams did not suck and our health care system was not a leaky sieve. Once we had our own retailers like Simpsons and Eaton's, and our most recognizable brands like Tim Hortons and Labatt had yet to be sold off to foreigners. Once a person could buy a book, musical recording, chair or pair of Stanfield's boxers in this land somewhere other than in a store the size of an aircraft hangar owned by rich Southerners. Once our national political ethos was not dominated by the kind of mean cant that used to make Canadian blood boil.

What I'm trying to say is that all progress isn't necessarily good. And when things go, they are gone forever. It's hard to imagine a day when we'll no longer be able to glimpse prairie tall grass. Just as the spirit sinks a little with the knowledge that at some point in the foreseeable future someone will lick the inside flap of a manila envelope, open a mailbox slot and send the last letter ever written by hand in this country on its final journey.

I mourn for other things too. The ephemera that you don't miss until it's just a wistful memory (a stubby beer bottle, a rum and butter chocolate bar). The bits and pieces that populate our collective imagination—grain elevators, lighthouses, drive-in movies, family farms, train whistles—bestowing context and colour on Canadian lives. Where, even, did the plain names we used to call ourselves—Bud and Clyde, Maggie and Ann—go?

One day I went to a library and pulled from a shelf a Canadian census from a century ago. It made a person wonder. What happened to the abrasive goods makers, the asbestics workers, the canal and commission men who then toiled in this country? Admittedly a hundred years is a long time, but where are the bill posters, the button makers, the liverymen, the gate and bridge tenders? What happened to the trappers, the matchmakers, the mica workers, the milliners and the pattern makers? Where, oh where, have the pork packers, the sash and door makers, the section and trackmen, the tanners and curriers gotten to? What in God's name has become of all those cartage men, pickle makers, yardmen and roundhouse men? Where did you go, you bleachers and bootblacks, you felt makers and fruit canners, you platers and pump makers?

If you're like me, you would be left slack-jawed upon learning that this country once had more conductors on trains than bank managers. That a century ago more people worked in boarding houses and hotels than built new homes in Canada. That this big land of ours used to have as many engravers and blacksmiths as miners. And that once hundreds of thousands of men in hats dragged sample cases from dusty town to frozen enclave, peddling their goods.

My next question is, have you ever met a "rectifier," a "notion maker" or a "huckster"? To your knowledge, have you made the acquaintance of a producer of aerated water; a crafter of axles, bags, boxes, brushes, carriages or cigars; or a manufacturer of feathers, glue, gloves, hammocks or lanterns? Run a finger down the list of "occupations of persons 10 years of age and over engaged in gainful employment, arranged in alphabetical order, 1911" and there they were.

Yet they're all gone now. As forgotten as buffalo hunters, town criers, cinder wenches, buggy whip makers and cordwainers. Leaving us all to wonder, who is next? Well, dear reader, the numbers again tell the story. It's a gloomy one for anyone with an attachment to the iconic, traditional ways of making a living. From 2000 to 2010 the number of fishermen in this country—a land first discovered by European whites when they came in search of cod—were expected to fall by 60 percent. During the same period nearly half of Canada's farmers were predicted to disappear. That decade was forecast to see an equal proportion of our fabled locomotive engineers finish their last ride.

The old trades are also dying, no question about it: tool and die makers (down 50 percent from 2000 to 2010); telephone linemen and ship's officers (down 35 percent); sheet metal workers, shoemakers and printing press operators (down 30 percent). In just ten short years typesetters essentially disappeared in this country. Au revoir, if things keep going the way they are going, barbers, boat builders and stockbrokers.

Sayonara, tailors and machine repairers. See ya later, people who wait on others from behind a desk, like travel agents and bank tellers.

⌒

IN my lifetime I've seen the pattern play out. My first real summer job was as a gas jockey at a Gulf Oil service station at a spot in mid-Halifax where a ganglia of roads met. It was years before I learned that service stations started out as adjuncts to general stores in Canada, and that gas would be put in buckets and funnelled into vehicles. Eventually service stations became roadside pumps, with an attendant on hand to dispense gas manually. By the summer of 1972, when I clocked in for the first time, gas jockeys were everywhere in this country. They wore coveralls with first names stitched on their sleeves and change belts around their waists. They filled tanks, pumped air into tires, cleaned windshields, and checked and added various fluids.

Having never worked anywhere before, I was a bad hire. I didn't understand that sitting down beside the gas pumps between cars failed to convey the kind of snappy image that a multinational oil company wanted. It helped not that the first time I lifted the hood of a car to check someone's oil was literally the first time I had ever gazed at the engine of a car. Or that my math skills were so rudimentary that at the close of some shifts my cash was off enough that I ended up toiling for almost nothing. Working at the service station still meant a little money and one of the first tentative steps into manhood.

That service station is a parking lot now. In fact, finding someone to fill 'er up at a gas station anywhere in this country grows harder with each passing day. The only human working at most service stations is inside, behind a counter or, sometimes, a glass window like a pawnbroker. If so desired, you don't even need to talk to a human at all: just swipe a debit card right there are at the pump, then go back about your business.

That got me thinking. One day I decided to make a list of all the jobs I had ever had. I stopped counting at twenty-two. What's interesting is that so many of them are completely gone or locked into some sort of unalterable death spiral. Oh sure, there are still hospital cleaners, Pinkerton Security guards, house painters, even a few assembly line workers. But paper boys have been replaced by car-driving paper "men" and "women." No one sells candy, shoes or toys for Eaton's for the simple reason that global competition put the department store out of business in 1999. Even the small independent retailers where I once toiled have been vapourized by the big-box stores.

My most interesting summer job was as a labourer for a ship's chandlery operation on the Halifax waterfront. I spent much of that single summer in a big rubber suit, clambering around inside pipes running from Halifax Harbour to the local power utility. My job was to scrape mussel shells off the walls of the pipes, then load the shells into the wooden box lowered from the surface. Did I mention that I was twenty-one years old and it was summer? Sometimes the sun was rising as I was getting in from the night's carousing. At noon I would wolf down my sandwich at the end of a waterfront wharf, then lower my head onto a pier and power-snooze for the rest of the lunch break as curious seals popped their heads out of the skanky harbour water nearby.

That ship's chandlery operation—like so many ships' chandlery operations—is long gone now; the site where salt-crusted scows used to dock for repairs has mutated into a high-end office tower. The newspapers where I've toiled and still work have to fight for every dollar. Circulation at *Maclean's*, the weekly newsmagazine, is about one-third what it was when I joined in 1988. At least it's still in business. So many of the Canadian magazines I once wrote for aren't.

Work, we all know, fulfills an economic imperative: things must be done and produced; a living must be made. But when the practitioners go, the skills themselves—often passed down person to person, forming a lineage that goes back to long-ago generations in distant countries—must eventually follow. That's lamentable for a whole host of reasons. Work steeped in long tradition is a form of living history. When the traditional talents disappear, a piece of our past goes with them. What's more, most Canadians want more than to trade labour for lucre. Writing some thirty years ago, Studs Terkel, the Homer of working America, championed the "search for daily meaning as well as daily bread" while one goes about one's daily labours. Meaningful work, Malcolm Gladwell declared in his book *Outliers*, must offer three things: autonomy, complexity and a direct connection between effort and reward. Which means there is only one possible conclusion to be drawn from the one in eight Canadians who, according to a recent poll, hate to get out of bed to go to work in the morning.

I can't say I'm surprised: BlackBerry-wielding wage slaves are always on; 4 percent of the Canadian workforce is employed in call centres, reading canned scripts. As the grandson of a man who went into the Cape Breton coal mines at eleven, I know not to romanticize how livings used to be made in this country. Technology surely makes jobs safer and more efficient. But I know this too: work defines us and is how most of us get our sense of esteem, accomplishment and competence. Equally true is that something is definitely lost when so much of work becomes mindless rather than thoughtful. The world becomes a lesser place when people who once found fulfillment in their jobs are being transformed into automatons rather than artisans.

⌒

THIS book is the quest to distill some essence of our shared experience through people who make their living the time-honoured way. By that I mean in a manner attached to the historic traditions, performed with the kind of pride that comes from doing something right and well, not just for the money, but for its own sake. I wanted to meet these people now because they are as endangered as the rare white-headed woodpecker. Like a Tilley hat–wearing anthropologist, I needed to see them in action in their natural habitat, because someday soon no one will know what a milkman or lighthouse keeper does in the same way we are puzzled by the notion makers and corwainers of olde. I wanted to observe those challenged breeds up close for the same reason that I wanted to talk to ranchers, locomotive engineers and travelling salesmen. The great forces of globalization, technology and what we have taken to calling progress are allied against them. Their time may be coming, just as it seems to be near for drive-in movie projectionists, blacksmiths and doctors who make house calls.

The reporting for this book took place in the early twenty-first century, when the world was everywhere in turmoil and flux. These, then, are really wistful dispatches from a distant era and a simpler time. The world has changed shape since then, and Canada with it. But the men and women in this book, in the way they make their daily bread, have stood still. (A bold asterisk must follow that last statement, since the breadth of occupations for women has mushroomed in recent decades.) Visiting those people is like having your life played back to you. They make memories rush forward and bubble up. You see your neighbourhood and your childhood unroll before you in someone else's experience.

The urgency is great, because as Daniel Gilbert, the Harvard psychologist, points out, we're reaching the end of nostalgia as the distinctive landscape of our past is replaced by a reality that is pretty much identical whether you're in Pouch Cove or Portage la Prairie. We all know there's no turning back in the midst of a transformation of the global economy every bit as significant as the Industrial Revolution. The factories close, the mines go silent, the last person who knows how to do something—catch a fish, fix a car, build a wall that's plumb—hangs up his tools and closes the door behind him. It's not a happy thought. That is just how these things tend to go. Which is why I need you to come with me now. There are a few people I want you to meet, while there's still time.

CHAPTER
ONE

ACROSS THIS LAND

NORTH from Toronto, through tracts of industrial land and suburbs, they made for the hard edge of the Canadian Shield. Past strip malls, telephone wires, barns, farmhouses and electrical transformers. Beyond cattle and scattered horses, homes where hard-working country folk slept and saloons where ne'er-do-wells lurked. From their perch in the glittering steel engineer's cab twenty feet above the standard-gauge rails, Craig Stead and Jordan McCallum have an unobstructed view of the frozen-in-time towns that snap by like postcards. The two men shift down and up. They hit buttons and pull levers. They talk into microphones and to each other. They look. They listen. They sound the horn. A couple of hoggers on the night train. Running the varnish into the black as the land changes from gentle plain to upturned granite.

Three hours ago their train hissed like a prehistoric beast in the rail yard of Toronto's Union Station. The Canadian tonight has eighteen cars plus the locomotive, each of them roughly twenty-five metres long. That makes the train shorter than the CN Tower then looming over its right flank but still four football fields in length. Plenty of room, in other words, to carry the 172 passengers waiting inside, amidst the Belle Époque opulence of Union Station, to Pacific Central Station in Vancouver, British Columbia.

The last time I was at Union Station, in the early 1990s, it was alive with humanity: commuters grabbing the GO train; jacked-up merchant bankers eager to spend their spoils in the alehouses of Yorkville; weary secretaries bound for the peace and quiet of the burbs. It was Toronto, so no one lost it completely. But people shoved and ran. Voices were raised.

Not like tonight. Granted, 8:30 p.m. is long past rush hour, and a lot of the traffic through the station is subway riders anyway. Still, I take it as symptomatic that in the busiest rail transportation hub in the country I can see only a smattering of humans amid the Missouri stone walls, the Tennessee marble floors, the Bedford limestone columns. Railways built this country. Confederation would never have happened without the Canadian Pacific Railway: British Columbia made a transcontinental railway a condition for joining the country. On the opposite coast, Prince Edward Island was only lured in when John A. Macdonald agreed to assume the huge debt from the island's own ill-fated railway scheme and promised a communications link to the mainland.

Before the CPR's completion Canada was a string of unconnected settlements separated by huge expanses of forest and prairie. The snort and hiss of the locomotive and the feats of the rail line's civil engineers—the 94.2-metre-high bridge traversing Alberta's Oldman River, the eight-kilometre tunnel through the Selkirk Mountains in British Columbia—became a shining symbol of what this new country could accomplish. The CPR tied the country together "like a line of steel from coast to coast," Pierre Berton, the author of *The National Dream* and *The Last Spike* told me once. "Our cities and towns popped up along it like beads on a string. Without it we would have developed vertically rather than horizontally. We became the nation we are because of the railroad."

But that was before two-car families and long-haul jets that could make it coast to coast without refuelling. People stopped taking the train. Freight, especially bulk commodities, became the dominant railway service. Built to create a nationwide passenger carrier similar to Amtrak in the United States, Via Rail Canada gradually assumed all of the country's main rail passenger services. But successive federal governments slashed funding. Twenty years ago Via cut its passenger network in half, axing some of its most crowd-pleasing runs. Today most of Via's traffic is on the commuter run in the Windsor-Quebec corridor. Even freight carriers have been closing stops in smaller cities to boost profit margins.

Still running, though, is Via's flagship train, a replica of the original Canadian, which made its first trip in 1955 and has been refurbished to harken back to the great age of rail. Its 2,775-mile route takes in most of Canada's scenic panorama. Who knows for how long in this age of quicker is better and everything must pay its way. That's why I was in the all-but-empty grandeur of Union Station, joining the trickle of passengers pushing luggage carts and pulling wheeled suitcases toward the check-in counter: the Asian tourists, the middle-aged woman with the T- shirt that said Don't Piss Me Off, the chunky brunette sporting a Swimmers Do It Better In The Water top, the trim old dude in a trilby and a tartan tie. Nobody—particularly not the guy with the middle part in the short-sleeved dress shirt who looks unnervingly like Dwight Schrute—is cool. They're mostly white and getting up there: men in sensible pants with elastic waists up around their nipples, ladies with plaster of Paris perms.

Maybe it's the anticipation of a transcontinental trip on one of the world's great passenger trains—perhaps it's happy hour at the Panorama Lounge—but they're also, to a person, exceedingly happy. Giggling, goofing around, their laughter ricocheting down the corridor. That makes them starkly different from the average wretched air traveller. This, in my view, is perfectly understandable. The trains run on time. A seagull never gets sucked into a diesel locomotive engine, causing the train to begin a death spiral five miles above the earth. At a train station no homeland security type stands before you, working his fingers into a rubber glove in anticipation of a body-cavity search. Instead a crinkly-eyed Québécois dude flirts with the ladies as he takes tickets and gets everyone organized.

At 9:30 p.m. they're allowed out into the yard: the "foamers" so ardent in their love for locomotion that they are alleged to foam at the mouth at the site of their favourite diesel train; travel buffs starting their first transcontinental rail trip; sufferers from fear of flying; maybe even a romantic or two looking for the kind of adventure that befalls men in tuxes and women in chiffon dresses aboard locomotives in Alfred Hitchcock movies. Every train I can remember being on also has its share of passengers susceptible to nostalgia for the sort of fabled, innocent past conjured up in Gordon Lightfoot songs and vintage Canadian National posters. People like that board the train vibrating with possibility. I know I do.

⌒

THREE days earlier Jordan McCallum walked over to the fridge in his Dundas, Ontario, bungalow. As a locomotive engineer who works the "spare board," he's the low man on the totem pole. Instead of a regular shift, he's on call seven days a week. It works this way: there's a list; first name in is first name out. As people are called out on the job, names rise on the list. Jordan gets two hours' notice when they want him to come to work. Back in the old days there were crew callers: junior guys who would jump on their bicycles, ride over to your house, knock on your door and give you your work assignment. Now someone just dials your cell phone.

"You can make the spare board work for you," says Jordan in a chipper voice, which I discover is his usual mode of communication. "If you're going to work with someone consistently, it's almost like a marriage. I like the variety. I like working with different people. It keeps it fresh. For me, until I have the seniority to hold a certain run, it just works."

So, he opened the fridge, grabbed his soft-sided lunch bag and threw in some icepacks for the sandwiches. Then he walked outside, got into his black Ford Escape and drove the sixty kilometres to the CN shipping yard in Mimico, in the southwestern part of Toronto, where he boarded a train for London. The next day he worked back to Toronto. A day later he awoke at the Comfort Inn on the outskirts of Sudbury, then took a cab over to the railroad town of Capreol, where Craig Stead—who he has shared a locomotive cab with on and off for fifteen years—had just arrived in his burgundy pickup. "When I started out, the Canadian's engineers were always old guys close to retirement," says Craig in his gravelly rasp. "They call the Canadian the 'varnish job.' When you're the engineer on the Canadian, you're 'running the varnish.' It was usually the reward for a long career. Guys like Jordan and me lucked out. All the baby boomers are retiring now. We know it's a great privilege to be an engineer on the Canadian."

At about 10 a.m. on June 9, 2010, they pulled the Canadian into CN's Mimico switching yard. They did their final checks. They grabbed their gear. Then they took a cab to the Marriott Hotel in downtown Toronto, where they snoozed, watched some tube and got a bite. By 7:30 p.m. they were back at Mimico, printing two sets of documents—their tabular bulletin general orders—off of the computer.

These orders let them know about washed-out track, broken rail or any other reason to watch their speed in the trip to come. Once they have a clear understanding of the route they call the controller and tell him that he can "release the train." Then they grab some earplugs and hand wipes and walk out into the clamour of the switching yard in the direction of locomotive 6412, one of Via's fifty-three F-40 class of locomotives.

It takes around fifteen minutes, backing up at a speed of twenty-five miles an hour, to travel from Mimico to the spaghetti bowl of tracks at Union Station. They pull into the east end of the yard. There Craig applies the handbrake and takes out the reverser, the train's "key," so the pair can head for the yardmaster's office to kill some time as the crew readies the train for its passengers.

The Canadian is an impressive hulk. The snub-nosed, twenty-year-old locomotive, with its three thousand horse-power that allows it to hit almost a hundred miles an hour; the swanky dome car and linen-service dining car where Hercule Poirot might have supped; the sleepers where you can choose from a berth like the one Marilyn Monroe climbed into with Tony Curtis in *Some Like It Hot*; the private bedrooms where you're dispatched to sleep by a motion that's partway between a rocking chair and some air turbulence. The lines are clean, the edges rounded rather than geometric. The overall look is comfortable, elegant and retro—not like those mean-looking bullet trains that rocket through Japan and much of Europe.

The thrice-weekly Toronto-to-Vancouver trip takes eighty-seven hours. Since Transport Canada prohibits engineers from working longer than twelve hours per shift, the journey requires nine crew changes. The two men entrusted with the first leg of the journey are dark-haired and of medium height, with the sunless pallor of people whose ancestors migrated to Canada from the British Isles. With nearly forty years on the trains between them, they almost certainly have the railway man's habitual gimpy knees—from all that jumping in and out of rail cars—as well as the progressive hearing loss that comes from working with a train horn mounted a few feet over your head.

They're in uniform: blue ball hats with Via Rail embla-zoned in yellow writing. (The traditional hickory-striped engineer's hats pretty much disappeared with the steam era.) They wear blue shirts and pants. (Only the freight guys over at CN and the guy in the Village People wear the striped engineer's overalls.) Both Jordan and Craig sport dark work-boots—Mark's Work Wearhouse, eight inches high with a steel toe and safety shank underneath—and railway-approved Bulova watches. The most striking things the two men have on are orange-and-yellow safety vests.

They travel light: lunches, shaving kits, a change of under-wear, socks, maybe another T-shirt. Via engineers must always carry a rules card, which states that they are qualified to drive a train and lists any minor physical infirmities, like the need to wear glasses. They also are never without their Via rule books, timetables and locomotive operating instructions.

What you won't find anywhere on their person is a cell phone or iPod. There was a time—long before either of these two worked their first trip—when the task of a junior man on a crew included a run to the liquor store before the shift started and, sometimes, lifting a shit-faced engineer onto the train. But not today. Nothing that distracts is ever allowed in the engineer's cab. Between the two of them Jordan and Craig have done this run hundreds of times. Their eyes are peeled. Their ears are open. Their minds are standing by. A train as long as a small town is in their care. Attention will be paid.

⌐⌐

THE engineer climbed into the cab first: round face, half beard that could be made of sand, a build like a decent junior league defenceman fifteen years after the last puck was dropped. Craig Stead, focused yet friendly, thirty-nine, grew up in Capreol, four hundred kilometres north of Toronto. There a person worked for one of two employers: the mining companies, which harvested some of the world's largest nickel and copper deposits. Or the mighty Canadian National Railway, which, when Craig was growing up there, sent thirty trains daily thundering across the tracks spanning Capreol's main street. Although Craig was the son of a mining company payroll clerk, his plans were a little different: after successive high school summers working for Ontario Hydro, he hoped to go to university to study electrical engineering. Instead, after high school he signed on as a CNR heavy equipment operator to earn tuition. He then spent the next six years servicing CN trains and rail lines throughout northern Ontario. "I kind of fell into railroading," he says. "By that point a lot of friends were finishing university. I had enough money saved up. But they were working for peanuts. I was hooked on the money. I decided to stick with it."

A restless guy who downhill-ski-raced in high school, Craig wasn't going to be content driving a crane forever. He transferred over to the "running trades," taking a job out of Niagara Falls as a conductor on the CN freight trains between Buffalo and Toronto. On freight trains conductors are the bosses. They look after the paperwork, operate the switch that allows the train to be guided from one track to another at a railway junction and perform a host of other duties. Eventually Craig moved to Toronto; then, tired of the big-city hustle, he took a transfer to the hamlet of Hornepayne, literally a thousand kilometres northward. The boredom kicked in again. "I wanted a change. I wanted to see a different side of things." So he signed up for engineer's training, which, once you pass the various aptitude tests, consists of two weeks of instruction in a locomotive simulator in a large mobile trailer.

Craig took a transfer back to Capreol, because of its proximity to Sudbury and its importance as a rail terminus, a more sought-after posting than isolated Hornepayne. But CN in his view wasn't what it once was. Before long Craig signed on to operate heavy equipment and run trains on the eighty miles of track at Inco's Sudbury nickel operation. When the mine went on strike, he heard Via was looking for an engineer to work out of Capreol aboard the Canadian. "I can't tell you how boring it was at Inco," he says. "I wasn't being challenged. I wasn't really using my skills. The job at Via was an opportunity to get back on the main line. I always wanted to be an engineer on the Canadian. So, I jumped at it."

The assistant engineer gets in next. At thirty-seven, he has a schoolboy's red cheeks and complexion. Craig, the pragmatist, may have taken to railroading mostly for the steady work and good paycheque. Jordan, slightly shorter and lighter, seemed to come out of the womb hankering for the touch of the throttle and the sound of the whistle. He grew up in Goderich, Ontario, but often spent summer vacations in Ottawa, where his grandfather had worked his way up to be CN Express's assistant terminal manager. The old guy was retired by then, but still liked to go have coffee with his cronies at the station. Often he brought his grandson along.

"I remember the first time I ran a locomotive," Jordan says. "I was eleven and the train had just come in from Montreal. They would cut the engine, uncouple it, then run up and fuel it and attach it to the night train—a two-car that would connect in Brockville with the rest of the train—then go right through to Toronto. I pulled the throttle. I released the brake. I rang the bell. I don't want to stay that it was magical. But you could do stuff then that would be off-limits nowadays. It was pretty awe-inspiring."

In school Jordan used to draw doodles of trains when he should have been thinking about the Treaty of Utrecht. On vacation he would go down to the end of his grandparents' street and peer through the chain-link fence at the trains on the way to the nearby station. Since he had memorized the time-table, he just had to look at his watch to know which train was passing. "I liked the sound, the smell. I liked the sense of possibility," he says. "When you go on a train, you go on a journey, and you never know what might unfold. I feel that way to this day. The excitement of departing on time and getting everyone where they are trying to go."

Because he grew up in the eighties and early nineties—when rail's day was already clearly done—people gave him funny looks when he confided his dream of following in Casey Jones's footsteps. To this day he has a thick stack of rejection letters from railroads throughout North America. Discouraged, he started punching the clock at a tavern in Goderich. On a whim, he sent out one last application. On January 4, 1994—Jordan has the date memorized—the phone rang. The Alberta Prairie Railway and Central Western Railway out of Stettler, Alberta, wanted summer help. Two weeks later he got another call: the Goderich-Exeter Railway in Goderich needed someone to help clean up the snow on its rail lines.

Jordan did that for a few months. In early April he jumped in his car. Three days later he arrived in Stettler. Home was an apartment on the second floor at the Big Valley, Alberta, train station. Jordan lived there for six months, sharing digs with another railroad man. During the day he kept his mouth shut and eyes and ears open and absorbed what he could from old-timers who started working the rails during the age of steam.

Mostly he worked on the freight short line—taking empty grain cars, waiting for them to be filled, then picking up the loaded cars and getting them to market. Sometimes, on weekends, he worked on the steam tourist train that made short excursions through the area. Six months later he was back in Ontario, getting his engineer's certification and starting a long run at CN Rail—toiling in the yards and as a trainmaster before going back on the trains as a conductor and engineer through British Columbia and Alberta and across most of Ontario. Then in 2009 a job opened up at Via Rail.

ⅽ⸱

IT'S comfortable up in the locomotive cab: plenty of head-room, warm enough for short sleeves, big enough for three grown men not to get in one another's way. A well-lit room with the overheads, the cream-coloured walls and the illu-minated dials and buttons. Noisy without tearing a hole in the tympanum. A pair of nice ergonomic chairs that pivot for a 270-degree view of the passing landscape through the bridge windows.

When sitting in the chair, the engineer can move the throttle—a little lever with a black knob on the end—up and down. He can flip the valve that pushes compressed air through the brake system. Craig shows me the dynamic braking arrangement that acts as a backup if the air brakes fail or the train hits an overly steep downgrade. He points out the power for the passenger area at the back of the train. Next to the throttle is the button he and Jordan punch to sound the horn.

Let me say right here and now that I like slang, the jargon of subcultures. Railway men have some of the best. Locomotives are called "hogs," which means engineers are called "hoggers" in central Canada and "hogheads" out west. In the Maritimes they're called "drivers," even though engineers don't technically "drive" a train—they "run" it. A caboose, when they still had cabooses, used to be called a "van," "crumbie" or "hack." Car men—those mechanics responsible for repairing and maintaining railway cars—were "car knockers" because they would frequently tap the underside of a freight car with a hammer, listening for defects. A conductor is sometimes called the "conny"; a switch man in a yard is a "yard ape" or "switch bitch." A "dinger" is a yardmaster. A machinist is a "knuckle splitter."

Years ago, railway crews were assigned a specific amount of work. The sooner you got it done, the sooner you went home. This was called working for the "cut-out." A "hose bag" is the line that supplies the air for the air brake system. "Do up the bags" means to connect the air line on the cars. "Tie it down" means putting a handbrake on the car to secure it. A train's maximum allowable speed is a "highball." If there's an accident, the investigation by supervisors is called "talking to the typewriter." "Running the varnish" means working on passenger trains, since they used to be given a fresh coat of varnish each year. Passenger trains, in fact, seem to be the subject of particular mockery: in some places a "baby lifter" is a passenger train brakeman. A "cushion rider" is a passenger train conductor. The electricity on passenger trains is known as "hotel power."

The Canadian's engines, like those of every Via locomotive, never shut off during fixed stopovers. That makes for a surprisingly quick getaway when the passengers are all aboard: Ivan, the service manager—the person who runs everything outside of the locomotive now that conductors have vanished in the cutbacks—gives them a quick briefing, they run a brake check, then switch the power from standby to normal.

Just before departure the phone rings. Craig listens, then hangs up. "There's a little problem," he says. "One of the passengers uses a breathing apparatus. His berth is too far from an electrical outlet for the cord to reach. Do we have an extension cord?" They puzzle about this for a minute or so until Jordan radios one of the yard control towers and lines up an extension cord that they can pick up on the way out of the yard. It is 9:57 when they radio the tower and say they're ready to go, on time, at 10 p.m. They get the all-clear. Jordan takes off the handbrake. Craig, eyes agleam, throttles up. The Canadian inches forward. The momentum of more than fourteen hundred tons is as absolute as that of a glacier.

The rail is standard gauge, which means that the distance between the inside edges of the rails is 4 feet 8½ inches. Most of the world's railroads, whether in Miami, Florida, or Novosibirsk, Siberia, are standard gauge. The United States—with 224,000 kilometres—has the largest railway system in the world. Russia (87,000 km) is next, followed by China (86,000 km) and India (63,000 km). Then comes Canada with some 46,000 kilometres, more than enough rail to circle the earth.

Rail still matters in this country. Canadian freight trains still move grain, coal, forest products and fertilizer materials from the west. From the east they transport minerals from mines and cars from auto plants. Almost all of that happens on rail lines controlled by the Canadian National Railway—which owns or leases 23,000 kilometres of railways—and Canadian Pacific Rail, which has some 13,000 kilometres of rail. Via passenger trains like the Canadian run almost exclusively on CN and CP track.

For identification's sake, track is split into subdivisions. After leaving the Union Station corridor, the Canadian travels along the Weston subdivision for a few kilometres before switching onto the Newmarket subdivision. Until fifteen years ago the Canadian used to be able to go straight up to Parry Sound on this line. Then cutbacks forced CN to streamline its rail network. Craig zigs, then zags the train until it is on a connecting track bound for Muskoka, Ontario's cottage country. Then he backs the train up to reconnect to another line so they can resume the journey north.

On foot Jordan supervises the operation at the end of the train. Afterward he climbs aboard and enters the train's park car, so-called because the cars are always named after a Canadian national park. People spend small fortunes to sit in these glass-domed cars as they ride across the country. Though midnight is near, a handful of them are up, having a glass of wine in the communal lounge area. Jordan and Craig don't get a chance to interact much with passengers. They've seen enough to know that people change once they're aboard a train. They loosen up. The tightness in their shoulders disappears. They volunteer intimate information easily to total strangers.

Perhaps it boils down to spending all that time together. Maybe it's the slow and easy rhythm. It could just be the sense of giddy unreality that comes from travelling across the land like a passenger on a cruise ship. Whatever it is, something about a train gentles the soul. Not just for the riders: seniors wave when we pass by. So do kids on bicycles and restaurant workers taking out the garbage.

One of the riders asks why they're going backward. Sometimes when asked this Jordan says he forgot his lunch or that his engineer's hat blew out the window and they're retracing their steps to find it. Jokes are made; laughs are had. The point is that the vibe remains undisturbed. Only then does Jordan start the trek back to the engine room.

Occasionally he has to move aside to let passengers down the narrow corridor between the sleeping cars, the small lounge and the snack bar. Jordan chit-chats with a steward folding napkins in the back of the dining room. A trip's on-train personnel depends on the customer count: a commuter train in the Ontario-Quebec corridor might have just one or two staff to look after travellers. On this trip twenty-six people are aboard the Canadian. Jordan passes half a dozen of them on the ten-minute walk back to the locomotive. Then he gets in his chair. It is time for the trip to really begin.

⌒

A ROAD map of Ontario, crowded with towns and bisected with highways and roads, implies humanity's crush. But the land empties out as the shining city of Toronto fades and the Canadian moves into some of the most iconic topography this country has to offer: the Group of Seven's boreal forest, sandy beach and Precambrian rock; the thirty thousand islands that pock Georgian Bay, a body of water big enough to be considered the "sixth Great Lake." A hundred and fifty years ago, when Ontario and Canada were going from hinterland to developed economy, the presence of a railway could bring a commercial boom to these towns that we pass—Midland, Port McNicoll and Victoria Harbour—and the ones where we briefly stop, like Washago and Parry Sound.

I've got a series of mental images that surface whenever I think about trains: the first CPR locomotive chugging into a place like Pile of Bones—so called by the native Indians but soon renamed Regina and the first headquarters of the North West Mounted Police—on the Saskatchewan veldt. A family of newcomers from Ukraine staring gogglie-eyed out the window at the vastness of this country as they prepared to open up the Canadian West. A whiskered conductor on the British Columbia line wondering whether Billy Miner, Canada's first train robber, would come swooping down at any moment.

In my mind I see gaunt-faced Ordinary Joes, collars up and cloth caps pulled low against the cold, riding the rails to the hobo jungles that sprang up around the big cities during the Great Depression. I see cheering throngs lining the roadside in places with weird-sounding names like Beavermouth and Hope as King George VI and his bride, Queen Elizabeth, made their forty-four-day trip back and forth across the country. Just as I actually saw tear-streaked faces along the rural towns and farmlands when Pierre Trudeau's casket made its slow way from Ottawa to Montreal to lie in state.

To me, trains have always been wrapped up in big events; they're about much more than getting from point A to point B. I understand that institutions have to be able to pay their own way. I realize that it is hard to justify a publicly owned rail line at a time when dead people sometimes sit undiscovered in hospital waiting rooms. But my heart sinks a little to think that someday the last train may haul ass across the arid prairie or through the primeval forest. That at some point in the not-too-distant future all the civility and joy will be squeezed from mass travel in this country. And all most of us will see of this vast land will be from thirty thousand feet in the air rather than almost at eye level, blasting through terrain otherwise untouched by man.

On the main line, which tends to be straighter and better maintained than the feeder lines, Craig can let the throttle out a bit. Not too much, mind you. On a straight, wide-open stretch between Toronto and Montreal a train can hit a hundred when the engine is opened up. At that speed, a passenger train the size of the Canadian takes fourteen football fields to stop. Farther north, where the rail bucks and weaves, climbs and dips, the Canadian rarely tops fifty miles an hour. Smoothness, not speed, is the goal of the boys in the cab. Precision is required when the front section of the train is going down a grade and the back end is going up and the whole structure—as many as twenty-four cars during the busiest part of the summer season—is curving east or west.

"The biggest part of being an engineer is knowing the road," Craig says. By "road" he means landscape. One aptitude test for becoming an engineer is landmark recognition: candidates are shown an image of some terrain for a minute or so, then quizzed about what they remember. The easiest way to recall when something significant is about to happen to a section of track is to fix it in the memory with a landmark. "We use lakes," says Craig. "We use streams and rivers. We use other things. There's a ridge over the Key River that lets you know when you're coming up to bridge and you'll have to have the brake on. When you're coming up to MacTier, the Highway 400 underpass lets you know that you have to slow down."

Knowing the road allows an engineer to react quickly and do the right thing at the right time: throttle up or down, apply the air brakes on each car of the train, hit the automatic brake if things have to happen really fast. The engineer wants to ensure the train is "spread out"—the cars far enough apart, the couplers with enough give—to limit the likelihood of something going wrong if anything unforeseen happens.

Craig and Jordan do more than watch the scenery. If a foreman working on the track or an engineer on another train has a problem that the engineers of the Canadian need to know about, he tells them over the radio. Every fifteen miles or so, the train goes over a defect detector—a heat-measuring device that does a temperature reading of the train's axles. If one is running too hot, Craig and Jordan will hear about that over the radio too.

An engineer, it becomes obvious, is a multi-tasker, keeping an eye on the gauges and meters, watching the timetable, planning for switches, crossings and other trains. A quarter mile from every road crossing stands a marker: a white square with a black W on CN rail, a diamond with a black W on CP property. When Craig or Jordan sees one, they punch the horn button—two long blasts, one short and one long, with the last one carrying the train right through the crossing. They hit the horn if they're near somewhere a crew might be working, or closing in on a bridge from which kids are known to dive into the river below.

At night, far from any sign of humanity, they blast the whistle every time they come upon a particularly curvaceous section of rail. Animals like to run parallel to train tracks. Engineers turn their headlights off and blow their horns loudly in the hope that the animals will just veer off into the woods. But trains still demolish wolves, coyotes and bear. They wipe out deer, moose and elk. They annihilate lots of dogs. "When you come around a curve, you have no idea what will be there," says Jordan. "Maybe rocks have fallen onto the track. Maybe a tree has been blown over. Because of the curve, you don't notice it until you're right up on it. Then you've got kind of a split decision to make. You're going to hit it anyway. But we're so much bigger than it is that we just plow through it and keep on going. Most of the time you don't even feel anything back there unless it is something significant."

The truth is that when things go wrong around a train, they tend to go really wrong. People get distracted. Men make bad decisions. Because of the size of the machinery, working on the railroad is unforgiving. Craig and Jordan can rattle off a list of friends and co-workers who lost legs when pinned by freight cars and feet when run over by coal cars. Some were crushed to death; others died in fires.

It's safer in the locomotive, but shit still happens. Every year more than a hundred trains—many of them carrying passengers or dangerous goods—derail in Canada, because of faulty equipment or rails, an engineer losing control or a train hitting something that wasn't supposed to be on a track.

Twenty-five years ago, twenty-three people died when a CN freight train and a Via passenger train collided head-on in Hinton, Alberta. An investigation found that human error caused the accident.

Sometimes there's just not much you can do. Every year about eighty people die "trespassing" on rail lines in this country. Transport Canada figures that about 10 percent of those deaths are clearly accidental. About 40 percent are obvious suicides. The rest fall somewhere in between: besotted men in ball caps who try to beat freight trains through crossings in their half-ton trucks; graffiti artists who choose to tag a rail underpass at the wrong time.

"You can't let it mess with you," says Jordan. "But it does mess with your head." A couple of years ago, he was working as a conductor on a trip along Lake Ontario. It was five in the morning and the sky was this incredible colour. Jordan was looking at the lake when he heard the engineer yell "Shit." A woman lay sideways on the track Superman style—body straight, hands pointing forward. Her eyes locked on the engineer's as the train roared toward her. "It's the noise that sticks with you," Jordan recalls, "like running over a bunch of hockey sticks. You could hear the wheel cut through the spine and hear the ballast [the gravel between the rails] being kicked up."

After the train stopped and the emergency call went out, Jordan's job was to walk back and find the body. He discovered the torso about half a mile down the track. Jordan had walked past the lower half of her body. Along the way he nearly stepped on one of her kidneys, which lay by itself alongside the rail.

UNLESS something is truly amiss, the engineer's job is short on heart-pounding drama. Some of it is drudgery. When the Canadian makes its two scheduled stops on the run between Toronto and Capreol—at Washago and Parry Sound—Craig and Jordan get out and hoist the new passengers' bags into the baggage car. Baggage handlers used to do that. But in the past twenty years railways have been doing more with less. The "fat" had to be cut.

A lot of the work, therefore, is rote. So much so that staying awake while riding through a landscape you've seen hundreds of times can be a challenge. Locomotives used to feature a "dead man" pedal that had to be pressed down by the engineer's foot at all times for the locomotive to function. It's since been replaced by the Reset Safety Control—an alarm that requires the engineer to manually press a reset button at a regular time interval, dependent on speed. The alarm starts quietly at first and grows in intensity. As long as the engineer moves the throttle, uses the horn or applies the brakes the alarm remains untripped. But if, for example, Craig fell asleep at the throttle and the alarm was allowed to sound for twenty-five seconds straight, the power to the engine would shut off. The brakes would kick in. The train, in time, would come to a full, wrenching stop.

Engineers, eager to prevent such a thing from ever happening, chug lots of coffee and drink lots of bathroom-break-inducing liquids. Lighting up a cigarette used to help keep guys awake in the days when you could smoke in a loco-motive. Constant eating can also stave off boredom and sleep, which explains why packing on the pounds is another occupational hazard of the railway man.

Mostly they talk to stay awake. They grouse about their employer. They gossip about co-workers, about who's in trouble with the boss, who just had a heart attack and—increasingly, given the aging Via workforce—who's got enough time in to retire. They lament the way the colourful oddballs who used to fill the ranks of the railway companies are retiring and dying off. They indulge in their particular form of gallows humour, which perhaps is best illustrated by the engineer who had hit an apparent suicide in the middle of a bridge.

Just before impact the man on the track turned around and smiled, the engineer recounted in a post-accident debrief.

"Then what did you do?" asked the investigator.

"Well," came the reply after a slight pause, "I wiped that fucking smile off of his face."

They talk about the game last night and the lady on the platform back at Union Station. Craig might wax on about his favourite mountain biking trail, Jordan his favourite ice-fishing spot. Sometimes they talk about music, since Craig is a drummer and Jordan likes to slap out some classic rock on the guitar.

The only train song he plays is by Ozzy Osbourne, and really isn't about trains at all. Knowing how many train songs are out there, I find that a little odd. One day I went looking online and found a collection of train-related songs compiled by Wes Modes, a California "sculptor, writer, performer, artist and mischief maker," who among his many interests "hops freight trains and gets in trouble." He had tallied up 550. His list includes "Midnight Special" (Creedence Clearwater Revival), "Engine Number 9" (Wilson Pickett), "I'm So Lonesome I Could Cry" (Hank Williams), "Mystery Train" (Elvis Presley), "Love Train" (The O'Jays), "Peace Train"

(Cat Stevens), "Marrakesh Express" (Crosby, Stills and Nash), "Midnight Train to Georgia" (Gladys Knight and the Pips), "I'm Moving On" (Hank Snow), "King of the Road" (Roger Miller), "Take the 'A' Train" (Duke Ellington), "Downbound Train" (Bruce Springsteen) and "Downtown Train" (the Mary Chapin Carpenter and Rod Stewart versions, but not the far superior one by Tom Waits, who wrote it).

He lists songs by artists like Jimmie Rodgers, Boxcar Willie, and Flatt and Scruggs, who seemed to do little else but write songs about hobos. Old blues yellers—Lead Belly, Son House, Big Bill Broonzy, Bessie Smith—loved trains as much as pasty-faced longhairs like the Rolling Stones, Grateful Dead and Neil Young. A lot of the songs are about disasters. Others are about movement—a train along the tracks, a man leaving something or heading somewhere. A very high percentage of them are about loneliness and longing.

One time I asked the late Toronto singer and guitar whiz Jeff Healey what it was about trains that engendered such great music. He talked about being a boy living in Brantford, Ontario, where he attended the local school for the blind, and the wistful feelings he experienced whenever the trains rolled past his dormitory. "I guess it's about being young with an imagination and thinking about being on these trains, going somewhere but never really sure where you are going to end up." Another time I asked Greg Leskiw, formerly of The Guess Who, if something about the train itself attracted rockers and bluesmen. "It's like a train is a living thing," said Leskiw, who by then lived in a house along the rail line in the south side of Winnipeg. "That rhythm builds and builds and it's so musical that you could go anywhere with it."

If you listen selectively, you can hear the entire rise and fall of railroading captured in those songs. The first train song I can remember hearing was "Canadian Railroad Trilogy" by Gordon Lightfoot, which pretty much set the standard for the mythmaking school of train tunes in this country. A quarter of a century later, Hamilton's Daniel Lanois wrote "Death of a Train": "We don't ride that train no more."

Craig and Jordan know railroading isn't what it used to be—and that things are unlikely to get any better. They understand that they won't be the last men to run a transcontinental train in this country. But they also realize that their breed is dying. They just shrug and go about their business. This job they have chosen is a way of life more than an occupation. It is no nine-to-five, home-in-time-to-get-the-kids-off-to-the-rink gig. The five-days-on-two-days-off shifts mean missed birthdays, dinners and other family Kodak moments. The uncertainty of the work schedule means friends simply stop calling after you back out of yet another barbecue invite at the very last minute. Always being on call means that you need to steal naps in the middle of the day when everyone else in your life is dying to do something, anything. No wonder the job is so hard on personal relationships: Jordan's marriage ended in divorce; Craig lives alone. "You get a lot working on the railway in terms of comfortable income, benefits and pensions," says Jordan. "But certain things get lost along the way."

Except I really don't hear much regret in his voice. Jordan is the romantic of the duo—the guy who never wanted to be anywhere other than in the locomotive, moving trains and people across this land. Craig, you get a sense, would have a far easier time doing something else as long as it kept him moving and engaged, mostly far from the city, in a way that involved big machines. Yet I want you to picture what I see at the end of their twelve-hour shift as we coast into the station at Capreol, where a crew change from Hornepayne awaits.

They are, remember, a pair of middle-aged men who have been working on the railroad for nearly twenty years apiece. And Capreol long ago must have ceased being an exciting place to stop. Still, there they stood—eyes glazed wih fatigue, joints creaking, stomach churning from rotgut coffee. The air was cool enough for long sleeves, but morning had broken twenty minutes ago. As they climb out of the locomotive onto the walkway, Craig moves his neck like a boxer loosening up. Jordan looks at the brightening sky.

"It's a great day," he says.

"Yeah," Craig says, "it's a great day."

CHAPTER
TWO

HOLY SWEET MOTHER

IN New Brunswick's Westmorland County a woman in green coveralls, a red toque and a pair of silver studs in her right ear stands inside a barn. Her serenity is extraordinary. Not just because swallows dive-bomb her from overhead and it is frigid enough that her breath forms sleet. Or because the barn echoes with the moos of 106 roaming cows—ropes of mucus hanging from their nostrils, distended udders swinging like a listing ship's chandeliers—overlaid with a noise like rain on a tin roof but that is actually torrents of manure and urine splatting on a concrete floor. No, I find the calmness of Dr. Jessica Harvey-Chappell impressive for this reason and this reason alone: I have seen athletes with seasons on the line, and watched police stand nose to nose with strikers. I have been in the room when politicians have told people who care that entire industries, probably their towns, are closing down. But never have I seen someone coolly trade farm-country gossip—what cows are yielding how much milk, who wants how much for what plot of land—while her arm is shoulder deep in the rectum of a dairy cow.

Jessica, from her calm expression, could be sitting in a nice ergonomic chair in an office somewhere, reading a report. With all her training she could be in a doctor's office, her name on the door, sipping a cappuccino between patients. She could be taking a day off at home, wondering what to pull out of the freezer for her husband, Les, and their two kids for dinner. Looking at her standing atop the overturned milk crate, you would not know that the barn smells ripe and that a few inches from her head a white Holstein cow with black spots like a Rorschach test is emptying her bowels in spectacular fashion.

Most of us live within a humdrum universe where a person's face becomes a sour knot if their iPhone dies. But this is the world Jessica has chosen, the life, for as far as she can remember, she wanted above all others. "I always knew I was going to be either a farmer or a vet," she says. In fact, she inhabits both worlds. And so, amid the noise, the smell and the flying fecal matter, patches of sunlight lather her forty-year-old face with fire, making Jessica look as serene as she does happy.

A staggeringly cold Wednesday morning. So cold that when Jessica pulled her truck—institutional grey with the green-and-white New Brunswick Department of Agriculture logo—into the provincial government parking lot at 8:30 a.m., she feared that the medicine in the modular insert on the back of the rig might freeze. She slapped the truck into park. Then she just left the engine running, as it would remain throughout her entire shift today, while she used her swipe key to enter the side door into the low-slung, regulation-issue government building. (When the weather is below freezing and she's got the truck at home, Jessica either keeps the truck in the shop with her farm equipment, as she did last night, or outside with the Bowie box insert plugged into a ceramic heater.)

The space inside the clinic is nothing special: metal filing cabinets, wooden desks, a glass window that opens to a counter where clients pay their bills, pick up medications and ask for advice from whichever vet is still in the office. A few touches let you know this is a veterinary medical office: posters of horse and cow breeds; the storage room with the stacks of medicine and supplies; the sawed-off X-ray machine, which she takes out to farm visits, sitting in the corner. Naturally, there are the requisite jars of weird animal fetuses: the foal that was only discovered when a dead mare was opened up, the pig with two sets of buttocks, the really long worm found in some animal's intestine.

Bernice Landry and Aline Mazerolle, the administrators who keep the trains running on time, were already in when Jessica entered, travel mug full of tea in hand. So were the trio of other vets who work out of the Moncton clinic: a pair of grown-up New Brunswick farm kids named Carl Dingee and Lisa Freeze, and André Saindon, whose words still carry the whiff of his Quebec birthplace and who is just months off from retirement. As she has done most days for the past eight years, Jessica removes her coat and hangs it behind the door in her office. Then she walks over to have a peek at the appointment book to see what's come in since she left the previous afternoon.

Jessica works for the Provincial Veterinary Field Services division of New Brunswick's Department of Agriculture, Aquaculture and Fisheries. That means that she doesn't see shih tzus and parakeets. She has never dewormed a pot-bellied pig, or had to put down a gerbil. Her world, like the world of her veterinary colleagues, is livestock—cows, horses, goats and sheep—that live, breed and die on the farms of southeastern New Brunswick. That makes them figures of historical import in this country. I say this because although Grand Banks cod and the inland fur trade may have brought the first European settlers to Canada, farming is what built it.

Farmers in these areas don't have to call Jessica or the others. But their services are cheaper than private clinics—for instance, they don't charge mileage on visits—and they will go anywhere to deal with a problem. They also offer 24-7 emergency service, something few private practices list on their website because it's hard work and not a moneymaker. Let me put it this way: rural private practice vets who make house calls are about as common as old-style country docs who show up in the midst of the snowstorm of the century. Which means that most farmers in the bottom left corner of New Brunswick can really only count on the four men and women inside this Moncton clinic, who, because their geographical districts tend to overlap, huddle for a few minutes each morning to ensure that all the calls get taken care of in the most efficient way possible.

Jessica, who wears her hair—brunette, with blond highlights—pulled back in a red elastic, is tall enough to have played college basketball. Her face, devoid of makeup, is open and friendly. She doesn't feel the need to fill the air. She listens.

When Jessica talks—despite her eight years of university in a discipline that's more difficult to get into than med school—it is not down to the listener. "It is hard to feel too superior when your arm is stuck inside a cow's rear," she likes to say. Also true is that you just don't grow up that way if your dad is a farm boy from New Brunswick and your mom a nurse from Manitoba.

Her parents met on neutral ground, Vancouver, when George Harvey's plan to work his way west had reached its natural conclusion. Somehow he persuaded the former Kristine Anderson to head back to the Petitcodiac River area of New Brunswick, where two hundred acres of good farmland could be had for the price of a cardboard box in an alley on the east side of Vancouver.

Their nine kids grew up feeding and milking the cows, slopping out the barn, bringing in the hay. Jessica, the eldest, was no hick: a good student, she played sports and had a social life. From the get-go she was also involved in 4-H, a mainstay of kid life in rural farming communities across this country. At the beginning of every year she got a calf from her dad's farm and was told she was responsible for feeding, washing and clipping.

"My favourite was a heifer named Jade. She was a really nice-looking cow," recalls Jessica, ready to hit the farm in her green sweater, tan vest and blue jeans. "We used to have a half-ton truck and a cattle box and we used to put the calves in the cattle box. We'd go compete locally at fairs around Sussex and Moncton. The top two would go to Provincials. And if they did well, they would get to go to the Royal."

If this sounds like a dreamy childhood, it was. Young people are deserting the Canadian countryside. When you grow up on a farm in New Brunswick—just like when you grow up in a Newfoundland outport or around the family store in rural Saskatchewan—most kids, in these early days of the twenty-first century, vamoose at the first opportunity. Yet, with one exception, all nine of the Harvey kids live in New Brunswick. They've also either followed their mom into health care in some way or are involved in farming like their dad, who at sixty-eight shows no signs of ever wanting to retire. Jessica essentially split the difference. She's a vet who works almost exclusively on farms.

ↄↄ

JESSICA, by her own admission, has "a heavy foot." So at a bracing speed we head through the flat New Brunswick farmland, past the silos and frozen ground, moving west from Moncton through the farm belt, where, except for university in Nova Scotia and Prince Edward Island and a few years of veterinary work in Alberta, she has spent her life. Each of the Moncton vets has their unofficial areas: Carl does Kent County, which is north of Moncton; Lisa handles the area around the university town of Sackville. André's small universe is the area between Moncton and the village of Salisbury, which is where Jessica's territory begins.

Her territory lacks wide-open space. Instead, it is mostly rolling hills, woods—pine, cedar and fir—and brooks filled with trout. Her domain includes the farming centres of Salisbury, Havelock and Petitcodiac, where she grew up, just down the road from Manhurst, where she now lives. She visits the scattered dairy, cattle and sheep operations and the horse stables. If a farmer calls and says he's got a sick cow or a mare that has foaled and things have gone sideways, Jessica goes, regardless of the weather or, when she's on call, the hour. "I measure everything in time," says the woman who nonetheless tells me that she puts fifty to sixty thousand kilometres a year on her truck. Using her preferred frame of reference, she might need an hour to get from one appointment to the next. Sometimes, then, she goes a little fast. "I've had a few fenderbenders," says Jessica, sun bouncing off her Ray-Bans, as she moves the wheel with the experienced driver's economy of motion. "But so far I've been lucky."

Right now we're headed for the village of Salisbury, about twenty-five clicks from Moncton, and a farm owned by people named Dykstra, one of the many Dutch farming clans in southern New Brunswick. The radio is on. Jessica likes a pop station with the call letters K94.5; a talk jock named Todd Vigneault is a guilty pleasure. But she's an incessant-enough channel surfer that the button has been worn smooth and shiny. "I listen to everything," she says. "I like to drive. If I've had a hard or a draining or a challenging call, sometimes the time between one appointment and the next gives me time to unwind."

This call, she tells me as she parks beside the red Dykstra barn, should be routine. As we get out, the eldest son emerges from the house, letting the screen door slam behind him.

"Where are Mom and Dad?" she asks.

"Inside," Martin-Dan Dykstra replies, "where it's warm."

Jessica gears up inside a comfortable room where milk is stored in big gleaming tanks. Her job, at its essence, is simple: to make farming operations profitable. Vets can increase a farmer's bottom line in two ways: by reducing illness and mortality and by boosting productivity. Both require a "herd health" program: an overall approach to preventing outbreaks of diseases such as mastitis and pneumonia or, saints preserve us, hoof-and-mouth or mad cow. But also by ensuring that in the case of cows, they yield lots of milk. For that to happen the cows need to get pregnant. Which is really why, on a day when the temperature with wind chill hits minus forty, Jessica is here.

She fiddles with the ultrasound machine and battery pack in her knapsack, then straightens out the loopy extension cord with the ominous-looking "rectal probe." Finally, Jessica pulls the goggles over her red toque and the straps of the knapsack over her shoulders. "It's Ghostbusters," she says, laughing. Then we head into the bowels of the barn.

Most veterinarians don't want to go where she is headed. Most new veterinary college grads would rather neuter pets in a nice city office than have to perform a less-lucrative Caesarean section on a ton of mare out in the sticks somewhere. There are a whole host of reasons for this shift. For one thing, there are fewer farm kids growing up around livestock and developing that affinity for large animals. As much as anything, the ascent of the female vet is what is doing in big-animal medicine. The first woman—an American—didn't graduate from a Canadian veterinary college until 1928. The first Canadian woman came eleven years later. But so much has changed since then: today women are the majority of the 250 to 300 graduate students from Canadian vet colleges. There's a lot of speculation on why this is so: for one thing, women's high school and undergraduate marks tend to be higher than men's. It's also just easier for women to get into veterinary schools than it once was.

Their unwillingness to take on large-animal work is partially a girth-and-strength issue. The new breed of female veterinarian also wants to be able to go home at five o'clock rather than head off to a frozen barn somewhere where a distraught farmer and sick sheep await. All of which means that female large-animal vets are a dying breed. New Brunswick's provincial vet service has only four: Jessica; her Moncton colleague, Lisa; a vet in Sussex named Nicole Wannamaker; and Olivia Harvey, who works near the town of Woodstock and happens to be Jessica's sister. As far as I can figure out, there isn't a single female private practice vet who exclusively handles large animals in the entire province.

Vets can do different things: they can research; they can try to keep outbreaks of infectious salmon anemia from roaring through fish farms; they can set the broken wings of owls. Jessica for the longest time wasn't sure if she wanted to be a farmer or a vet. But once she decided, it was big-animal work or nothing for her. "I did not want to do any small-animal practice," she says. "It's just not my thing. I find it too intense and emotional. I think I'm caring and compassionate, but small-animal medicine is too over-the-top for me."

For a time getting there didn't look good. Her marks at the Nova Scotia Agricultural College in Truro, Nova Scotia, where she did an animal sciences degree, were decent (an 85 average). But the Atlantic Veterinary College in Charlottetown only accepted thirteen New Brunswick students a year. When Jessica didn't get in the first year, she moved back to her dad's farm in Petitcodiac and worked there while she upped her grades. She kept applying. "The first couple of years I tried to get in, the college was more geared toward small animals," she says. "The year I finally got in four people interviewed me. Three of them were large-animal vets."

⌒

THE Dykstra farm is a "free stall" operation. Unlike "tie stall" setups, where cows are kept in one stall and milked there, the Dykstra cows are free to wander around the cavernous barn between milkings. When they're ready to milk, they sashay into the "parlour," a series of raised platforms with gates that prevent the animal from moving. Martin-Dan or one of his family wash and clean the cow's udders before the milking machine is attached. When the milking is over, the farmers clean up. The cow just walks out. Both types of farms have advantages and disadvantages for vets: tie stalls are usually smaller and a bit warmer. Free stalls, Jessica says, tend to be big steel structures, which means that on days like today they are a whole lot colder.

When I wasn't looking, she pulled a long sleeve over her left arm. It resembled one of those orange cellophane packages in which your paper arrives on a rainy day. Martin-Dan is scanning down his clipboard at the list of cows that he wants her to examine. Usually he marks them with paint before she arrives. "But today I'm apparently a little early, which never happens," she says in a teasing way. Jessica starts to slowly work her orange-sleeved arm into the rectum of the first cow that requires her attention. The process is a visceral one: as she goes, she cleans out the waste with her left hand. Vets, it turns out, always use their non-dominant arm for the procedure, since once upon a time they jotted notes with their good hand throughout the examination. Over a radio somewhere in the barn John Mellencamp sings the praises of being born in a small town. "You feel for certain features in the ovaries," Jessica explains. "Through the uterus you can tell what stage she is at in her heat cycle or how far along in the pregnancy so that the farmer can manage her lactation." Ultrasound images of the inside of the cow appear on her goggles, helping her to complete the picture.

This cow is "open," which, in the parlance of the dairy farm, means not pregnant. The next one isn't. The one after that is. The stoic Martin-Dan doesn't change his expression either way, even though the longer a cow is open, the less money a farmer makes. Jessica passes the information on without editorializing as her fingers roam among the cow's innards. She talks constantly, in her unhurried way, as she works. The woman is by nature friendly. It's also part of the job. "At first it was hard to multi-task," she says. "I'd be concentrating on the job—checking the cow or horse—and I wouldn't be talking this much. But as I got more experienced, it got easier. You're always doing something and talking to the farmer at the same time. The farmers want you to maximize your time while you're here. The meter's running, remember. Plus, they're farmers. They don't see a lot of people. So they love to talk."

Their lingo makes sense: cows that have just calved are "fresh"; those that have taken a rest from milking, as happens in the two months before they give birth, are "dry." If everything is going well and the task doesn't demand too much of her attention, Jessica troubleshoots, talking diet and nutrition and vaccinations with her farmers to head off troubles before they begin. It's a two-way street; if Martin-Dan has concerns, he tells her. Jessica looks at a cow with a bad hoof, which they decide to keep an eye on. Then Martin-Dan leads her to a stall holding a thin-looking cow and her calf.

"She hasn't been eating well," he says of the cow, which has ribs that show. "She's pretty lethargic." They manoeuvre the animal to the side of the stall, where a gate keeps her still as Jessica does her physical. She listens to the heart, lungs and abdomen through a stethoscope. Then she plunges her hand into the cow's rear end and gropes around to check some other organs. The news is bad, the diagnosis unequivocal: a heart murmur. The farmer asks if anything can be done. When Jessica says no, the cow's fate is sealed: one way or the other the cow will be put down, probably to become hamburger.

By the time Jessica is back in the milk house, stripping off her gear, she has probed by hand the guts of a dozen cows. Only six of them are pregnant. There's a cloud over Martin-Dan's face. On Jessica's advice he's been using an artificial insemination program called Ovsynch to get the herd reproducing and keep the cycle of milk production going. "He's discouraged," she tells me. "But those are normal results. Maybe the cows have been working hard at milking and not working at breeding. There could be fertility issues. It's hard to know. Martin-Dan is just very enthusiastic; he wants to do a really good job. He wants them to get pregnant." They work through his options. It takes a few minutes, but she talks him down; he'll give the program another shot, he says. Jessica, who has taken off her messed-up coveralls, is using a heavy-duty spray to clean her gear. Through the steam, I see her smile when Martin-Dan announces his decision.

~

BACK in the truck she tells me that she's probably at this farm once a month, about average for her "clients." Sometimes farmers think they can handle whatever has happened by themselves or with a little advice over the phone. Other times it's "better get over here fast because all hell is breaking loose." Breached deliveries. Colic. Gashed-up legs. Pneumonia. A host of maladies can befall a farm animal. "Take your prolapsed uterus," Jessica says, a term with which I am not familiar. It means that while calving, a cow has somehow pushed her uterus outside of her body. In January, when there are lots of beef cattle calving in the area, Jessica runs into a fair number of prolapsed uteruses. "Some are easy—some are hard. It's got to go back in. So I give the cow an epidural and I start pushing. It's this big bag that has carried a calf. It can take forty minutes of pushing; my arms ache for days after. The whole thing is a bloody wet mess. I put a calving suit over top of the coveralls. But I still get wet. There's a lot of blood from the afterbirth. I'm covered in blood and water, and it's all happening at the back end, so I'm covered in that too."

C-sections, another regular procedure, sound like no walk in the park either. Jessica describes the circumstances of her most recent one: a farm that had lost its power during a big windstorm and a cow trying to calve, with a twisted uterus preventing the birth from taking place. Jessica used a local anaesthetic to numb the "surgery site." She sedated the cow and then cut a fifteen-inch-long hole in the animal's side. "I reached into the abdomen, pulled the uterus out and made an incision. Then the farmer and I pulled the calf out." That understates the process a little. The calf weighed about a hundred pounds, which explained why Jessica couldn't untwist things. By the time she stitched up the uterus and incision ninety minutes had elapsed. A "difficult" C-section can take two and a half hours.

We pull into an Irving Big Stop, where she has arranged to hand off some medication to a farmer. Jessica punches the office number into her cell phone. "Hi, I'm all done at Dykstra's," she says. When Jessica hangs up, she explains that a while ago her colleague André stitched up a high-spirited filly with considerable difficulty. Now those stitches need to come out. Carl, who is already out at the stable, thinks that this is more than a one-person job. Jessica, lucky her, is closest.

A car finally pulls up. A window rolls down. The farmer's two-month-old calf isn't drinking much water and just lies there. Jessica asks a few questions. They settle on a treatment that is about sixty dollars less than the medicine he was originally scheduled to pick up. "If things get worse, call me ASAP," she says. Then she slaps the truck into drive and is back on the road again, bound for the Maritime Saddle and Tack Shop a few kilometres east.

Inside the barn, the horse's owner, Michelle Bourque, leans up against the stall. Styletto—shiny chestnut coat with a white-patched forehead and dabs of snow on two legs—has quite the lineage: sired by a dressage world champ whose daughter sold for a cool 2.5 million euros at an auction, she's on the market for twelve thousand dollars. But even to my untutored eye Styletto—chest heaving, nostrils pulsing—looks skittish. She's a hoity-toity show horse that spends her time cantering around exhibition rings. Nonetheless, when Carl tries to pick up the stitched right front leg, she rears up, smashing her head on the barn roof and making a sound like someone chopping wood. "Whoa," says Carl. "Whoa," says Michelle. "Whoa," says Jessica.

Injuries are unavoidable for big-animal vets. Horses kick. So do cows. Mostly it's just bruises and bangs. But André has never quite recovered from being bitten in the face by an ornery mare on what should have been a routine call. Horses will try to stomp you with their hooves, as Styletto aspires to do to Carl at this very moment. If your arm gets wedged in between a wild horse and the sides of the stall—as seems to be on the verge of happening to Jessica, now also inside the stall with Styletto—it could get fractured. Styletto, it is decided, needs a little sedation. Jessica heads for the truck. She returns minutes later carrying a black case with silver latches and hinges that snap open.

Inside her emergency kit are needles, syringes and IV catheters. Rompun, an injectable sedative, is in a 50 ml bottle, about half the size of the ampoules of Flunazine, a painkiller. The Dormosedan is in a clear bottle with labels on either side. Because Styletto is so jumpy, Jessica puts a little of it together with a little Torbugesic, another sedative. She flicks the syringe a couple of times with her index finger to get the medicine flowing. Then she steps inside the stall.

The horse isn't big. Even so, Carl clenches Styletto's halter for control. Amid beams of light from a flashlight, Jessica, making calming noises, searches for the horse's jugular vein with her left hand while the syringe stands ready in her right.

Inside an eight-foot-square stall a wrestling match ensues. A chorus of "whoas" fills the barn. The vets muscle the horse. Styletto, moving counter-clockwise, muscles back. Somehow Jessica gets the needle in, plunges the sedation into the horse's circulatory system, then backs off to let it work.

The drug combo, under normal circumstances, should take the fight out of a horse. Styletto just stands there. "It's the animal's temperament that's the issue," says Jessica. "Taking out the stitches isn't that painful. It's just that nothing we were doing was to her liking. It's just her personality. She's very stubborn." The vets look at Michelle. Michelle looks at them. Carl tries to grab the filly's right leg and then just gives up. In her mind, Jessica is already mixing Dormosedan and Rompun, a more potent sedative combination, and reaching for another syringe.

⌒

BACK in the office half an hour later Jessica plucks a doughnut from a Tim Hortons box. If she doesn't eat something now, she might have to go the entire workday with nothing more than a few handfuls of trail mix from the plastic bag in the cab of her truck. She's had half an hour of downtime. Now a horse is about to foal. Dairy cattle tend to calve all year. Horses tend to foal in the spring. This, for example, will be the first equine birth Jessica has seen this season. Normally when horses foal, a farmer doesn't reach for the phone to call the vet. But this couple raises show horses.

Maryanne Gauthier, who also works for the local John Deere dealer, focuses on paints, so called because of their distinctive markings. Her husband, Marc, raises Clydesdales, just like in the Budweiser ads. Marc is a farrier, which means he shoes horses for a living. He's also a bit of a worrier. He's spent a lot of time and money on a mare named Amelia Earhart. So when the mare's water broke, Marc hit Jessica's cell phone number and told her that, if possible, her presence would be appreciated.

"There's a good chance it will all be done by the time we get there," says Jessica, back behind the wheel. A cow can take two hours. Horses are a lot faster. That her water has broken implies that she will foal in the next fifteen or twenty minutes. "But there's no happy medium with foals," Jessica says. "They're either really easy going, or it's really, really hard."

We're heading southwest from Moncton, down an unremarkable stretch of Trans-Canada Highway before turning off onto a country road. The Arctic temperature seems to give everything outside a hard, metallic look. Jessica's cell rings: "Have you seen any signs of heat . . . I can book something for next week in the morning . . . Oh, I know Lola. What's her due date again . . . I'll call you later when I have my book and we'll make an appointment."

The community we're bound for, Havelock, sits at the junction of Route 880 and the Hicks Settlement Road. When I look on my iPhone, I note that the settlement—along with towns in Nebraska and New Zealand and streets in Singapore and Kanpur—is named after a British general famous for putting down an uprising in Raj-era India. The Internet also tells me that Havelock's most famous citizen is an evangelist named George McCready Price, known for his creationist thinking.

I personally believe in evolution. However life comes to be, there is no mistaking the wondrous yet messy path of the natural world inside the barn where Maryanne, dressed in ladylike pink, leads us. Paints in stalls line either side of the barn. Amelia's space is the last one on the left. She's not alone: kneeling in the hay, a fifteen-minute-old Clydesdale foal blinks from the shock of entering this here world.

I may have gasped. I may have thrown my hands up in the air like a three-year-old coming down the stairs on Christmas morning. I can't really recall. All I can relay for certain is my abiding sense that city folks don't often get the opportunity to see such things, and recall the way that foal looked—eyes barely open, white forehead, muzzle twitching, I imagine, in confusion—and how his mother, covered in blankets to keep her warm after the exertion of birth, just stood there obliviously munching hay.

A horse like Amelia is probably worth fifteen to twenty thousand dollars. So I understand why Marc, kneeling by the foal's side, is so excited. He reaches up to shake my hand, then goes back to cleaning the foal's coat and whispering encouraging words. Jessica, at this point, just stands by the entrance to the stall watching things unfold. Marc and Maryanne try to get the foal to rise, fail, then try again. Finally, on the shakiest of legs, it gets to its feet. "Holy sweet mother, look at the size," says Maryanne. The horse, now about forty minutes old, reaches almost to her shoulders. Marc looks like he may weep with joy. Jessica makes an appreciative noise and notes the time: 3:06 p.m.

Foalings are supposed to follow what she calls the "one-two-three principle." If all goes well, the foal is supposed to be upright within an hour. Within two hours of being born it is supposed to be feeding. An hour later the mare is supposed to clear the placenta, which at this moment hangs a foot or so out of Amelia's rear end. If the placenta doesn't clear by this time, the danger of infection increases. Jessica watches Maryanne and Marc try to get the foal to latch onto its mother to feed. Then, after a while, she opens the metallic case.

She lifts out a vial of oxytocin, the hormone responsible for producing the uterine contractions that birth the foal and push out the afterbirth. She pops the needle of a hypodermic syringe into the centre of the ampoule and draws out the medicine. As Marc calms the horse, she hits the jugular with the needle, plunging the medicine into the Clydesdale's bloodstream. Then there's nothing for her to do but watch and wait.

⌒

JESSICA does not text. She does not look at her watch. She doesn't sneak out to the warmth of the still-running truck to call the office. She just stands there waiting for the contractions to start rippling through the mother. The barn is Jessica's natural habitat. By my calculation, she has spent the equivalent of nearly two years of her life ministering to barn animals since becoming a vet. She just can't escape the agrarian life. Her husband, Les, a Prince Edward Island boy whom she met at vet school in Charlottetown, works for a dairy equipment manufacturer based in nearby Sussex. Lesley, their nineteen-year-old daughter, who's studying to become a licensed practical nurse in Moncton, went through the 4-H ranks. William, the five-year-old, is also following in the family tradition. When Jessica gets home—after dinner, homework and some cleaning up—she'll walk out onto her twelve-acre spread in Manhurst and head for the barn, where they keep a few head of beef cattle, some horses and sheep. This is Jessica's notion of fun.

Inside the Gauthier barn, therefore, she is calm, she is cool. With Marc's help she ties off the foal's umbilical cord, cuts it, then applies iodine to the horse's "outie." Once the foal begins to suckle, all attention focuses on Amelia. Oxytocin acts fast, but only for a short time. The first three doses are spaced twenty to thirty minutes apart. The hope is that eventually the mare will kneel in the hay and naturally expel the placenta. Jessica pulls out a bit more of the afterbirth by hand. The pink membrane still only hangs a couple of feet outside the horse. She ties it into a knot in the hope that gravity will drag more of the placenta out. At 4:06 Jessica gives Amelia another shot.

If in an hour's time things haven't moved along, she will hit the horse with another dose. If that doesn't work, Jessica will have to remove the afterbirth manually. Otherwise, Marc's beloved Clydesdale could develop one of several nasty-sounding complications, each ending in "itis," any one of which could kill the mare.

Thus, here Jessica stands, face unclouded by doubt, as if she has all the time in the world. This isn't just some commercial transaction between strangers. Marc and Maryanne aren't just "clients." Jessica's home is a couple of minutes away from this place by car. Their daughters went to school together. They're neighbours and therefore are accorded the mutual respect that such a relationship deserves.

This was how it once was in this country. Don't you remember when we all had that sense of community and connection? I don't just mean in a business-employment sense, although before the Net and the global marketplace everything was local: if you made something, chances were that you sold it to someone you went to elementary school with. The parents of the kid who centred your peewee hockey line hired you to fix their toilet, balance their books and rotate their tires. The guy who had lunch once a week with your dad's first cousin hired you for a job you had no right getting because, well, you were the son of the first cousin of the guy he lunched with four times a month, fifty-two weeks a year.

It was, for better or worse, as though we all lived in this same small village in which we each had a shared urgent responsibility for the other residents. When good deeds were done, people didn't tweet about it or demand to have their names put on a building. I thought for a second about K.C. Irving on the way to becoming the third-richest non-monarch in the world, who spent a Christmas Eve driving through a blizzard with a couple of bags of road salt to help a stranger stranded in this same neck of rural New Brunswick in which we now shivered. He was seventy at the time. But he lived in a place and time where corner stores still let customers buy groceries on credit and delivered free to seniors. Back in the day teachers stayed late of their own free will to coach school sports teams. Doctors made house calls.

Now get sick, go broke or bonkers or otherwise fall by the wayside in a Canadian city and you'll find out who has your back. Sometimes it seems that we may as well be in the wilds of the Arctic. If you suffer the big one while walking down the street in broad daylight, I hope that your old elementary school teacher—not some fresh-faced family physician worried about "liability issues"—is passing by.

So it does my heart good to know that in certain places in this country the "we're all in this together" spirit still lives. Make no mistake, standing here and waiting is part of Jessica's occupation, for which she is decently compensated. But there are easier ways to make a buck than being a country vet. She never wanted just a "job," she says. Jessica wanted something more than a mere exchange of labour for lucre. "It is a combination of things," she says when I ask her what it is about this work that appeals to her. "I grew up on a dairy farm so I like cows and horses and find working with them rewarding. I like helping farmers. It's a symbiotic relationship. I need the farmer and the farmer needs me and we need the cows and horses. It's an important industry. I wanted to be part of it and this is how it worked out."

We're back in the truck now. Amelia has received her last dose of oxytocin. There's nothing to do but see if it kicks in. Jessica is going to pick up her son, William, at his babysitter's and then drive me back to Moncton, where my rental is parked. William comes out of the house wearing a big furry hat with earflaps. "I think I know him," he says of me to his mom as he climbs into the back seat. "That can't be the case," Jessica starts to say. But it's been a long day and the little guy's out already. And so we drive, K94.5 filling the car, through this country where she knows not just the people but the cows and horses by sight.

Delirious from hunger, I'm imagining an artery-narrowing Angus Burger at the McDonald's I know is just a few minutes from where I parked my car. Jessica, who has already put in a day that's as physical as a stevedore's, hasn't had a full meal since breakfast. A half an hour from now, when she returns to the Gauthiers', she hopes to discover that Amelia has dropped her placenta. Otherwise, this woman has miles to go before she eats, let alone sleeps.

It's not like there are really options. Somebody has to do it. Somebody has to slide open that barn door with frozen fingers and keep watch until these folks she knows so well are in the clear. That she might say the hell with it and head for home is out of the question. It has never entered Jessica's mind. She has been training, in one way or other, for this moment her whole life. These are her people. This is her world. It will take as long as it takes.

CHAPTER
THREE

THE MILKMAN COMETH

BILL was fretting. If his neurons seemed hyperactive, they had reason to be. In his mind, he pictured hangdog kids gazing at empty cereal bowls. He saw seniors, their porous bones softening on the spot. He visualized bakers, feet up, reading the day's *Chronicle Herald* as their mixing bowls sat idle. He imagined coffee drinkers at Tim Hortons drive-throughs, gape-mouthed upon learning that a medium double-double was suddenly as accessible as lasting peace in the Middle East. "Oh man I'm late," whispered Bill. "I'm late." And so he arrowed east, his white van careering forlornly through the gathering dawn, his eyes scratchy with fatigue, his gut clenched with worry.

He had been on the job for six hours by now. The workday began at midnight at the Farmer's Co-Operative Dairy at the dead end of a country road outside of Halifax. The day was meant to end in the early afternoon, twenty kilometres from where he'd started, after presenting his last cases of milk, yogourt, cheese and cream to a restaurant readying for the suppertime rush. But halfway through the workday things had gone sideways: the chef at a retirement home slept in; when Bill Bennett Jr. finally pulled into the parking lot and unlocked the door leading to the kitchen, he was a full sixty minutes behind schedule.

A milkman's enemies are legion: blizzards, gridlock, meter maids, leaky fridges. Time is the ultimate foe when you have somewhere around two hundred stops a day to make and a route that reaches from the newest suburb to the oldest corner of one of the country's longest-lived cities. "You think you're okay and then there you go," Bill moans. "Oh my, oh my. I knew this was going to be a bad day soon as I got up. You know what? I was right." Lose a couple of minutes on each stop and the interminable day extends even longer. What's worse, the problems grow exponentially. When Bill is late, his customers—the stores, restaurants, nursing homes and other wholesale stops that make up 90 percent of his income—start looking at the clock. If he simply didn't show up—well, you never know, the entire Halifax Regional Municipality might just clank and hiss to a halt.

Today all Bill had to do was conjure up 3,600 mislaid seconds from thin air. Hard to do when your timetable is already as tight as a Hank Williams lyric. When you are sixty-one years old, operating on six hours' sleep, beset by tennis elbow and carpal tunnel syndrome along with a host of other physical maladies. So, you hunch a little lower over the steering wheel. You narrow your eyes. You crank 101.9 FM a little louder on the dial, listening to announcers who sound like they've had the same kind of life experiences you've had. Then you blow through town as the streets unfold before you, and you search for slices of lost time.

For a decade Bill has arrived at my house at around 5:30 a.m. every Tuesday and Friday to drop off a few litres of one percent milk. Occasionally, when the kids were babies or if I had to catch an early flight, I'd glimpse his truck out there idling in the street. I never once saw his fleeting shape between truck and doorstep. For ten years we've communicated by worn pages torn from a notebook, scraps of paper or a used envelope filled with crabbed writing. Usually he was informing us that we owed him money, that a holiday was coming up or that he and his wife were actually going on vacation, which, he explained, they seldom did.

It always made me feel guilty and a little sad to get these messages. Sometimes I'd stand on the step, hold the piece of paper in my hands and try to imagine what this man who made the calcium appear looked like. I didn't know then that our lives had been intertwined for half a century. That his father, Bill Sr., used to deliver milk to my parents when I was growing up a couple of blocks from my current address. I can't remember laying eyes on him either. I just took his existence for granted, like the Tooth Fairy. My parents left tickets or money in a glass bottle on the front step. The next morning there'd be milk.

I was a boy of my time and place. Sometimes, when sleeping in a tent in someone's backyard, we'd get up in the dark before the Bills, Jr. and Sr., arrived. Then we'd skulk through the streets looking for milk money to steal. A decent score would mean a bottle of Mountain Dew, a roll of wine gums, maybe even a round of Fudgsicles. Milk, though, was what packed muscle onto our adolescent frames. At the kitchen table, I'd pour it into an Esso service station glass that urged car owners to Put a Tiger in Your Tank, then I'd empty it in one gulp. I'd drown my Raisin Bran until the fruit bobbed in the wake like baby seals. I'd run through the door, hair plastered to my forehead from some kids' game, yank the fridge door open and just chug straight from the bottle.

I reached for the milk jug for practical reasons: milk was cool and refreshing. It was not water. All these years later I wonder whether there is something infantile about milk's attraction. Or whether a human body just naturally has a hankering for all the calcium and protein that led some marketing genius to label it "the perfect food." I just know that the weight, texture and taste of milk—along with the feel of corduroy and the first few bars of the theme from *Get Smart*—never fail to transport me back to a time when a thirteen-year-old still pondered the great riddles of the universe: Who's tougher, Captain Kirk or Gordie Howe? What exactly were SpaghettiOs? Betty or Veronica? And that when my time comes—when I lie in a bed unable to conjure up a few words to describe what the whole strange experience has been like— it is my firm belief that the taste of milk may be one of the few shards of memory still ricocheting through my hollowed-out cerebrum. Making Bill Bennett a perfect entry in a book such as this.

BILL Bennett Jr. told me to wait under the big skim milk sign that marked the turnoff to the Farmer's Dairy. "Be there at 1:40," he said. That way, after getting the day's load, he could pick me up in his van before starting deliveries. "You'll know it's me because my name's on the side in big letters," he told me over his cell. Usually Bill travelled alone. Which meant that once he had quickly rearranged the front of the van, my seat was an overturned milk crate covered by a blanket, to the right of the driver's seat.

"I could have done anything," he said. "My mother's mom had some money and she said she would pay for my education. But I got my grade ten, then stopped because I hated school, every second of it. That was around, let's see, 1964. I had been working with my dad since before I could remember. So I started working with him in one of those old flat-nosed DIVCO vans." You can see the miles in his face: the skin around his pale eyes, cross-hatched and wrinkled from all that staring into the dark; the grey flecks in his brown-red beard; the nose bent like a Bedouin chieftain's. He radiates the kind of weary pride I've seen in five-hour marathoners, union organizers and bar-band bass players.

Bill says he's five foot ten,, but he looks shorter. After four decades of humping his dolly up and down stairs, through restaurant basement passageways and across convenience store parking lots, he's got a permanent slouch, as if forever shouldering some unseen weight. Bill jokes about having a belly, though I don't detect one. On the other hand, anyone can see what he means when he talks about having "bumps" on his hands from all those years of handling cold stuff without gloves.

Today he's in his "uniform." Greenish fleece, blue T-shirt, navy work pants. Black shoes, like the ones old-time basketball referees used to wear, a blue Niagara Falls ball cap. The big surprise is his voice. Not so much the rasp, as unexpected as that is for someone who has reputedly never smoked a cigarette or drunk anything stronger than chocolate milk. I was expecting someone taciturn, maybe who had even lost the power of speech after all those years of working alone in the dark—the way that fish living deep in the ocean are blind because they no longer have the need to see. Truth is, this boy can talk. "Is what I do important?" he barks. "I never thought about it, but oh God yeah. People need milk, so why not do it? I've hurt myself many times. Falling down steps, I twisted my ankle. I never missed a day even when I had spinal meningitis. I went in and helped out. I even went to work when I had kidney stones, and you know *they* hurt. Forty-one years and not one day missed. It takes a man to come out and do this all day for twelve hours. That or a dummy—one or the other."

The tumble of words, I suspect, just makes him feel less alone out here in the dark. At two o'clock in the morning, city bars are just starting their second act. Police stations, emergency rooms and all-night convenience stores are busy. In the suburbs and bedroom communities most people are dreaming. Outside, the world is filled with a humming silence. No car, dog or human moves. Lit by front-porch bulbs that someone forgot to turn out, twenty-first-century streets look like an Edward Hopper painting: cool, soft-focused, as if some revelation is at hand.

I get the distinct feeling that even if I weren't here, Bill would still be addressing his sleeping customers, the moon, even his own product in the back of the van. The monologue, out of necessity, is his dominant conversational form. He snorts at the inequalities of life, grouses a little about his lot and rants a bit about his pet peeves (traffic cops, competing dairies, lousy drivers). By nature, though, he is an infallible optimist, a buoyant spirit who believes "you have to take the bad with the good" and that "things will turn out all right in the end." An effervescent personality who likes to punctuate his upright words with a "ha-ha-ha-ha," the occasional "mama mia!" or an "ay, caramba" like Bart Simpson.

When he feels really good about things—and sometimes even when he doesn't—he can't contain himself. "Dad had a good voice," Bill says. "He used to sing in all the choirs and sounded just like Bing Crosby. I've got a good voice too. He was Catholic, Mom Protestant. I used to sing in both churches every second week. But that was years ago when I was young and foolish." Nowadays he does a lot of his singing on the job. In the run of a day you might hear him sing a cappella snatches of "Yellow Submarine," "Love Me Tender," "Downtown," "It's Hard to Be Humble" and "Over the Rainbow." Or he might join in on songs from the radio that only a country music aficionado could know. (If you wanted to conjure up someone from that world he resembles, think Merle Haggard—proud, weary and just a little pissed off.) Sometimes, for no obvious reason, he gives the words a reggae inflection or makes them sound like Count Chocula is singing them. Other times he sings words that seem a little silly: "Ten little turkeys all in a row. One little turkey said I don't know"; or "Giddy oh, giddy oh, giddy I oh. I smell the blood of an Englishman." When I ask him about the improvisations, he shrugs: "I make up those lyrics. I make them up all the time. I make them up and throw them out. I'm always singing and acting the fool. My wife says, 'Will you be quiet—all you do is sing or whistle.' I say, 'Be happy that I'm happy.'"

The first time I hear him sing—Kenny Rogers' "The Gambler"—it is in an octave high enough that I steal a glance to see if he is serious. We are heading west into a small residential enclave that is more rural hamlet than city suburb, so Bill drives with impunity on either side of the street as he searches for his customers. He rolls down his window, then from the van shines his big, boxy flashlight on the mailbox or front window to see if the red-and-white Farmer's sign is face out (Delivering Convenience Right To Your Door) or reversed (No Thank You!). If the house is running low, Bill slams the van into park, climbs out and scuttles around to the back of the vehicle, his gruff monologue trailing behind him in the night air.

His ride is nothing special: sides white and unadorned other than with his name; the roof flat except where broken by a sloping refrigeration vent. The cab, where he sits, littered with an empty plastic oil bottle, used Tim Hortons cups and the tools of his trade: sunglasses, an alarm clock, an invoice printer, a blanket and some rain gear. End to end the van can't be more than twenty feet long, and is utterly devoid of glamour. Which in that respect doesn't make it much different from the oldest picture of a milk wagon I could find when I went looking one day in the Nova Scotia archives. The black-and-white photo showed a hollow-eyed middle-aged man—not unlike Bill— sporting a moustache like a push broom. The old-timer wore a peaked miner's hat, jacket, vest, tie, dress shirt, cuffed trousers, and workboots. His buggy seat was probably six feet off the ground. The horse was big. So were the wheels. Milk cans filled the back.

This was before refrigeration, when iceboxes were literally boxes with ice, providing little storage. One of the enduring memories for the people of Dartmouth, Nova Scotia, would have been the clip-clop of Rod Morash's horse ambling by memory from house to house to drop off bottles of fresh milk and take away the empty bottles from the day before. That and the trail of steaming "road apples" deposited in the street, letting people know that the milk wagon had passed their way. In those rough days most of the necessities of life—meat, fish, laundry, ice, vegetables, bread and other things—were delivered person to person by horse-drawn wagon. Progress was coming though. By 1918 the photographic record shows enclosed milk carts that afforded the driver-owner some comfort and more storage. A few years later the vans seemed worthy of minor royalty: the carriages white with elegant dark trim, the spoked wheels less clunky, the horses bigger, better kept, more regal.

When Bill Bennett Sr. climbed onto a Twin Cities milk wagon for the first time back in the midst of the Great Depression, a horse still hauled his wagon over the cobblestones and dirt roads of Halifax. Corner stores didn't really have refrigeration equipment. Supermarkets were still ahead. That left milkmen, even if the old horse and wagon was already on the road to obsolescence. The experience of Borden's Farm Products in New York City was illustrative: in 1928 Borden's operated 3,025 horse-drawn routes, requiring 3,697 horses. By 1946, while handling roughly the same number of customers, it was running only 168 horse-drawn routes, with just 181 horses in its stable.

All of which is to say that twenty years later when Bill Sr. started bringing milk to the DeMont household at 1681 Cambridge Street in Halifax, he was behind the wheel of a motorized van. An accountant who grew up in the same neighbourhood as I did remembers him as a wrathful, glowering figure who seemed to like to yell at any kids who inconvenienced him. That doesn't square with the popular mid-twentieth-century image of the milkman: the smiling guy in the crisp white uniform who arrived glass bottles jingling in metal baskets, then left with the slam of the milk box lid.

They were always more than just deliverymen. In the early days many of them would keep a house key and put the milk, eggs and cheese right in the cellar icebox, and later in the refrigerator. They would help in other ways too, leaving food out for a dog or cat, reaching something on a high shelf for an elderly customer, changing a fuse for an ill-equipped housewife. They apparently aided housewives in distress in other ways too. Every joke in the surprisingly large genre of milkman jokes runs along the lines of this one I found after about thirty seconds of perusing the Internet. A man and his pregnant wife go to the doctor, who mentions a new treatment that allows a female to transfer the pain of childbirth to the father. The couple decides to give it a shot. The mother is hooked up to the machine. The doctor starts it up. The mother starts to feel better, but the husband doesn't feel anything. Puzzled, the doctor turns up the machine. The mom's smile grows; the husband reports no change. The doctor keeps cranking the machine: the woman feels very, very happy; the husband just shrugs. Eventually they go back home and walk up to the front of their house, where the milkman lies dead on the front step.

Bill Bennett Sr., who worked twelve-hour days and was married to the same woman for forty-five years, had no time for servicing bored married ladies. By the time his only son started tagging along on the route Bill was driving a step van, so called because of the ease with which it allowed the driver to step in and out from behind the wheel to make deliveries. It was built by the Detroit Industrial Vehicle Company. DIVCO produced trucks for bakers, laundrymen, even paper boys. In the 1950s and 1960s, anyone who delivered anything probably drove a DIVCO truck. Starting in 1937 until production ceased in 1986, DIVCO trucks were essentially designed the same way: an all-steel body, a bumper-less, streamlined bulldog front, a drop frame that allowed the driver to drive the van while standing instead of expending all that energy getting in and out of a seat.

My guess is that Bill Sr. drove a Series 1 DIVCO van, the main milk truck on North American roads during the late 1950s and early 1960s. It packed a six-cylinder, seventy-five-horsepower engine. The controls, including the throttle and brake, were on the steering wheel. When packed to the roof, it could hold fifty-seven cases of milk bottles. Pedal to the metal, this model could near fifty miles an hour.

I never saw one drive anywhere near that fast. I remember them anyway. I was a child then and the world I recall—the clothes, the homes, the avenues, the storefronts—was pretty much the one I see when I look at old pictures of DIVCO trucks today. The street is always empty, it is always Saturday morning and the sky is forever streaked with blue. Nothing bad has ever happened and no one anyone loved had ever died.

I'm not alone in this fantasy. At vintage auto shows all across North America, cars nuts ignore the sparkling Mustangs and Corvettes and surround stubby, reconstituted DIVCO milk trucks. They ooh and aah about the paint jobs, the movable seats, the classy grill, the vintage AC systems that blew huge amounts of cool air into the yawning interiors. Then their eyes glaze over in a haze of desire as they rhapsodize about bygone days. "You take a DIVCO to a car show, it always draws a crowd," Les Bagley, director of the DIVCO Club of America, which has 750 active members nationwide told me. "You could have a '57 Chevy sitting right next to it, and it would still draw a bigger crowd."

⌒

NOWADAYS Bill Jr. drives a Ford van with a V-6 351 engine under the hood. At about two tons, it is a fraction of the size of the one his dad drove in the 1960s and about half as big as the one Bill himself captained in the eighties. Vans are shrinking out of necessity: declining family sizes mean fewer kids and fewer kids mean fewer milk drinkers. Juices, power drinks and designer coffees have eaten into milk's market. As well, most of the recent immigrants to Canada come from countries where milk has never been a traditional drink. The upshot is that Canadians now drink about half as much milk per capita as they did twenty years ago. But it's the rise of the supermarket that really killed the milkman. In the United States, 80 percent of retail milk sold during the 1950s was home delivered. Today it's less than 1 percent. In the United Kingdom and Wales, doorstep deliveries now account for 10 percent of milk sales. No such exhaustive statistics are available in Canada. But it's safe to say that the downward slide has been just as precipitous here.

In 2008 Farmer's Dairy employed six hundred people, but very few of them delivered milk. Farmer's, which started in 1921, at that point had just seventy to eighty vans delivering its products across Nova Scotia, Prince Edward Island, and Newfoundland and Labrador. The dairy is a farmer-owned co-operative, which means the profits go back to the farmers who produce the milk. That's admirable. But it also means that drivers are independent contractors who are paid a volume-related commission and don't receive a salary, paid vacations or any other benefits.

The hard-working ones, like Bill and his wife, Blanche, do okay. "Let's put it this way," he says as we head for the top of Clayton Park, a leafy, established Halifax suburb. "Each one of those cases is worth four dollars and this van is loaded to the back five days a week. I could buy a motor home for sixty-five thousand dollars. I bought this van. I bought another van. I own a house and a camp. I didn't finish high school, but no one in this family has ever wanted for everything."

He parks, jumps out, opens the back doors and climbs into the back of the van, which is separated from the front by a partition. A tinfoil-like insulation lines the walls, which are otherwise adorned only with a 2009 printing company calendar. The refrigeration system hums, rattles and cools. The boxes of product reach to the ceiling and extend right out to the doors. (In the fall of 2009 the Farmer's line included various kinds of milk, cream, yogourt, juice, sour cream, margarine, butter, cheese and various other spreads.)

There's nothing haphazard about the loading process: the night before, Bill calls in his order to the dairy. At midnight a forklift carries his load out. Single-handedly, he fills the back of the van in the order in which he expects to unload it: first the big boxes of cream and yogourt for the waterfront restaurants that he will visit at the end of the day; last the one percent milk for the homes in Hammonds Plains at the start of the route. All told, it takes one hour and twenty minutes to load the van up. The hardest part of a long, physical day.

In a perfect world, because of such loading precision he wouldn't have to shift cartons around after hopping into the back of the van. He wouldn't have to squeeze himself into impossible spaces. He wouldn't have to contort his body to reach things that weren't where they should be. He would simply grab the first box he saw. Then, like a running back hitting a hole, he would cradle the milk in the crook of his arm and take off in a bandy-legged trot up the driveway. The first time I see him do this I think he's showing off. But he jogs back too, marks something down in his worn-out scribbler, then guns the van a ways down the street, stops and does it all again.

Like many of us, there's part of Bill that loves the night. The way stars glitter and how sounds—the rustling of trees, the buzz of an electrical transformer—expand to fill the air. Most things and people look better in the dark. The mundane becomes mysterious, sad, maybe even a bit magical. Before the streetlights blink off, for example, Bill might glimpse a raccoon waddling across a lawn or a deer kicking through the leaves. Once he found a drunk lying in the middle of the road and called 911 for the person's own good. Another time he got rousted by a police squad car after asking a girl walking along the side of the road whether she needed help.

Don't get the wrong impression: if this part of the world is any indication, home milk delivery is now mostly the indulgence of comfortably off, two-income families willing to pay extra for the convenience of not having to drive to the supermarket. Cars with plenty of warranty sit in the driveways. Though wilderness lies at the end of the cul-de-sacs, chaos seems distant and unknown. From these homes hours from now husbands, wives and schoolchildren will emerge, flinging on their coats, blowing kisses and slamming doors.

It will be 5:30 before a few early-morning joggers and the occasional paper boy—now, of course, a middle-aged man or woman—start to materialize. Until then Bill's only company are the hurting songs on the radio and the counter folk at the doughnut shops where he stops for his many coffees—usually in a travel-go mug and always three creams and no sugar ("I'm sweet enough!")—a quick pee and some small talk about assorted thoughts and concerns: "Damn, Bill, you seen the construction up by the overpass?"

Today it is clear and dry with the temperature in the low single digits. But summer is definitely over. You get the feeling that you'd better grab the good days while they last because the Nova Scotia winter approaches. We drive down hills so steep that on icy winter days his brakes have given out, letting his van slide into ongoing traffic. We glide into dead ends that stop so abruptly they surprise you. As we weave through subdivisions that I didn't know existed, modest prefabs and spruced-up century-old homesteads

materialize in the van windshield. We pass an old cemetery. Then seconds later creep down a street of tract housing
without sidewalks, where no Egg McMuffin wrapper has
apparently ever blown.

When people think of this country, the impenetrable
Canadian Shield and veldts of undulating prairie may come
to mind. The truth is that four out of five of us dwell in
urban enclaves strung out along the Trans-Canada Highway,
trying to raise a family in a place where meeting a mortgage
doesn't require the sale of a kidney. Connection to the broader
community is hard in places so young. Human contact is
fleeting amid suburban sprawl where people seldom move
around by anything other than car and scant places exist where
neighbours can actually meet.

Know that I'm nostalgic, not wistful, about my childhood.
The reality was that it was necessary to talk to a few people in
the run of a day: the guy behind the meat counter, the light
meter man, the bank teller, the lady handing out stamps and
penny candy at the combination post office—five-and-dime
store up the street. Now it's possible to run your daily errands
with an almost total lack of social interaction: you can pump
your own gas and bag your own groceries. I now buy most of
my Christmas and birthday presents, books and CDs online. I
personally make 99 percent of my cash withdrawals through
an ATM and, increasingly, pay my bills online.

I know, I know. Out in the burbs where Bill today works,
a postman still slides the mail in with a click through the
letter slot. Someone folds up the daily newspaper and flings it
on a front step. The Internet, though, is already on the verge
of making those folks obsolete too. Anyone can see where

we're headed: all this cutting out the middleman may make economic sense, but even commerce, on some level, is about more than just dollars and cents. Something is lost when simply pointing and clicking can accomplish everything that needs to be done in the run of a day.

Bill may not know the names of all his customers, but he knows their addresses, their order numbers and their tastes. Some have been customers for so long that he finds himself rummaging through the back of the van and getting their order without even thinking. With the insomniacs he exchanges small talk born of a mutual fondness for the time between night and dawn. The bed-bound slackers like me get the occasional note. That's still a more real human connection than a disembodied voice from a call centre in Mumbai.

At a time when customer service means a big "how d' ya do" from the Wal-Mart greeter, it does the heart good to know there are still guys like Bill here. It's more than yearning something that provides a fluttery feeling behind the breastbone, reminding you of childhood. Milkmen aren't museum pieces. They do something essential at a time when much of what passes for work lacks value or is so far removed from the people it benefits that the link is impossible to make. Ask Bill if he feels "fulfilled" and he just shrugs. After all these years he's come to hate the brutal days. And no one would confuse what he does with the utilitarian art of the craftsman.

But spend a little time with him and the complications of his job are obvious: the juggling of orders and coddling of customers, the creative problem solving, the muscle power and stamina, the mastery of time and space. It's hard, demanding work and Bill is good at it. "I could work fewer hours," he says.

"But I want things done right. I want things done a certain way. If that takes a little longer—well, then it takes a little longer." Bill likes being his own boss. And dealing with customers gives him a kick. In his work—as for his father before him—there's also a direct relationship between effort and reward; the more milk he delivers, the more money he makes every week. "Do I find my work satisfying?" he asks, repeating my question. "Yeah, I guess you can say I find it satisfying."

⌁

BILL is still trying to make up lost time as he pulls his fully loaded dolly up the nineteen stairs to the downtown pub's door. Inside, a talk radio jock and The Guess Who blare in competition over the rattling and wheezing of an industrial kitchen. He moves stiffly around in the cold locker, humming as he rearranges the shelves to make room for cream, milk and sour cream. After doing some quick calculating, he bustles back outside and climbs into the van. "I can't get at the sour cream!" he exclaims. "Boy, did I goof. Sour cream, sour cream, where are you?"

It's light by now. Spring Garden Road, one of Halifax's main drags, looks the same as any other major thoroughfare in a twenty-first-century Canadian city: a young Asian woman in a tailored suit clicks by on high heels; a woman in an Islamic head scarf makes change at the newsstand; a twentyish guy—trim as a nail, olive skin—fiddles with his iPod as he steps past the panhandler sitting on the sidewalk. If Bill turned in a circle, he would see a Turkish restaurant, a brew pub, a martini bar, a cell phone store and a bookstore with Malcolm Gladwell's latest thumb-sucker in the window. A film company with an Academy Award under its belt is headquartered not far from where Bill rummages. Within a couple of blocks of his van—which has a handwritten cardboard "Farmer's delivery van" sign in the window—a hot yoga class is under way and someone is buying a single espresso that costs as much as this book.

Years ago I lived in a well-off section of Toronto. Occasionally I would see a middle-aged man in Old Country peasant clothes walking through the neighbourhood, ringing a bell and pulling a small cart. He was Italian, I was told by one of his countrymen. A knife sharpener now living with a daughter, perhaps; a man who longed to be back in his old Sicilian village practising a trade passed down from generation to generation.

The scene was totally incongruous, like he had stepped through a crack in time. And I get a bit of the same feeling watching Bill, still doing a job that hasn't essentially changed in 150 years. Civilians pay no heed as they walk near him. If they knew he was a milkman, passersby might stop, rub their jaws, say "Really?" and smile at the very quaintness of the notion. Tom Cruise doesn't star in movies about men who wear ball caps, smell of bad milk and use the service entrance. Nevertheless, Bill and the kitchen help, cleaners, deliverymen and other nameless folk who work behind the scenes in the service industry allow our everyday lives to function with a semblance of order. Our ignorance of what they do shows how well they do it.

This responsibility digs furrows into Bill's brow. At 10:30 a.m. he's still running late. To make things worse, instead of printing bills, his printer voids them, wasting reams of paper. "There's not enough paper. Not even close," he moans after another botched attempt. "I don't know what I'm going to do. Why did I take my spare paper out of this van? Oh man, the paper I'm going through. I don't have time for this. Man oh man, what else can go wrong?" Soon he finds out. As he's on his knees filling a refrigerator in a mall convenience store, the owner leans over and tells him that he's completely out of milk at two other outlets he owns farther down Bill's route.

You can see the walls of the store narrow and feel Bill's pulse begin to pound louder. A year ago he lost the illusion of invincibility. One day Bill's face went numb, he suddenly started to drool and couldn't speak. His doctor said it sounded a lot like a stroke. He fit all of the criteria: early sixites, stressed, a few pounds overweight. Night work of any kind is bad for the health. Women who work the night shift have higher breast cancer rates. Night shift workers are at a higher risk of accidents, sleep disorders, bone fractures and digestive problems. Scientific evidence even shows that the disruption of the body's circadian rhythms can make a person's metabolism go haywire and lead to hormonal and metabolic changes that even increase risks for obesity, diabetes and heart disease.

Bill's tests were inconclusive. Even so, he decided to do a better job looking after himself. On the dashboard sit a nice juicy apple and a heart-smart bottle of water, plus the alarm clock he uses when he has time for a short nap in the cab. "I know I can't do this forever," he says. "But I'll keep doing it until I can't do it no more. I've been paying into RRSPs for years. If I have to stop, I'll be okay."

We shall see. Bill likes to fish for trout at a lake near a backwoods cabin he owns with a friend. He plays golf. Once he was a good enough ten-pin bowler to compete in tournaments in the United States. For now, all the fun has to wait until retirement. After his twelve-hour days Bill heads home and has a bite in the bungalow he shares with Blanche and their two grown-up children. He watches a little television—"I have no interest in sports, news or politics, but man I love karate and kung fu movies"—and is in bed by six. Six hours later he rises and does it all again. On the weekend mostly he rests.

It took chronic back trouble and two knees badly in need of replacement to get Blanche to quit working. Now Bill is searching for his own exit strategy. They're debt-free; if they watch it, their savings should see them right through old age. He just has to find someone willing to take on his route. Because these people need their milk. For nearly five decades that duty to his customers was something for Bill to hang the entire workday on. His daughter, a sculptor and children's centre worker, and his son, who works in retail, have eschewed the family tradition. He can't just quit.

Bill is joking when he asks me if I'd ever be interested in giving the job a shot. Too physically hard. Too many hours. Too much of the wrong kind of stress for someone who gets all flustered if an editor sends an email asking where the heck the story is. The end may be drawing nigh for jobs like this. But what finally wipes the garden-variety milkman off the face of the earth won't just be the vagaries of economics; it will be because people willing or able to do the job no longer walk the earth.

I ponder the apparent inevitability of this as we plunge deeper into Halifax's business district. We stop at a caterer's, a steak house, a hotel dining room, a tourist shop and a faux Italian trattoria, where Bill moves like a ghost past all but his service-economy kin. By now, his mood has lightened: the invoice machine is working again; he's bummed some printer paper off a passing Farmer's van. The back of this truck is finally clearing out, making it easier for him to manoeuvre around. Somehow those lost minutes are being found. "I'm happy, oh I'm happy again," he sings before breaking into an "O Canada" expansive enough for hockey night at Maple Leaf Gardens.

There are still all those empty fridges to deal with farther down the line. But you must take the good with the bad in this kind of work. Bill moves milk. It's not finding a cure for cancer. Nor is it ever likely to be on some magazine editor's list of "jobs of the future." A pessimist might see him as the last of a dying breed. Bill says, "Not yet, buddy. Not yet." Then he punches the van into drive and clatters through the weak afternoon sunlight. The bleary-eyed guy who brings the farm to the citified kitchen table. The beat-up working man who feeds my family. Nobody is ever going to erect a statue to a man like Bill Bennett. But I have to tell you: after all this time it's a pleasure to finally make his acquaintance.

CHAPTER
FOUR

WATERING HOLE FOR DREAMERS

BY the time he heads south on Broadway Avenue, Stu Cousins, a man of ritual, has walked the dogs. He has breakfasted. He has sat in the swivel chair before his desktop computer. There—on his favourite bookmarked websites— he has checked the buzz on the new releases in the long list of musical genres that he favours. If he likes what he reads, Stu points, clicks and listens to a couple of cuts. If he likes what he hears, he places an order. Either way he brews a chai tea in his travel mug. Then, on gimpy knees, with music playing in his head, he exits right out of the front door of the eight-hundred-square-foot house that he shares with his wife, Dayna Lozowchuk, their four hound dogs and their six thousand records and CDs.

Stu veers left at the corner of Broadway, which even in late morning has more diverse life forms than you'd expect to see on a commercial drag in a former temperance colony. Plying his migratory route, he waves, says hi, occasionally takes in a little neighbourhood gossip. For seven blocks he walks at the nice clip of a man who spent a couple of decades jumping when clients said jump but who now has the luxury of acting in a manner that acknowledges that things that really matter don't have to be rushed. At a point where the Saskatoon traffic convenes coughing and wheezing from three different directions he stops.

Stu reaches into his pants pocket and pulls out a key. It's nearly eleven. But, as he notes, "vinyl collectors aren't known for being early risers." So, no one is standing there waiting at 628-B Broadway as he unlocks the glass door with the metal security grate. From the entranceway the fifty-three-year-old pulls a sign adorned with Bobby Dylan's mug onto the sidewalk, proclaiming to the world that the Vinyl Diner is open for business. Then, in brittle prairie air, he stands tall, a touch stooped and a bit on the angular side. An empathetic face dominated by dark-rimmed glasses, straight lips and a nose that tapers. From a couple of pictures rounded up on the web I know that Stu, at some point, wore his brown hair short and blunt. Today it's shaggy and swept eastward, more front man for The Sheepdogs than account manager for Saatchi and Saatchi, which is what, in fact, he used to be.

Stu looks around. He observes. For a couple of seconds he takes in the traffic speeding by toward the airport that commemorates Prime Minister John G. Diefenbaker, and the football stadium named after hockey immortal Gordie Howe.

He watches cars and trucks head toward the bridge across the South Saskatchewan River to the booming downtown where the mining companies that give the provincial economy its snap are headquartered, and out toward the highway leading west to the ghost towns left when the rail lines stopped running. Then, as he has done Monday through Friday for the past sixteen years, he heads up the stairs.

Past posters for big-name acts and artists I've never heard of, he walks over skanky carpet where the smell of pipe tobacco mysteriously lingers. The higher he climbs, the more the vintages of the artists on the walls recede in time. Until, at the second-floor entrance to the shop, a man who bought his first LP at a Woolco department store at age thirteen faces the covers of albums that hit the stores before he could ride a bicycle: *The Times They Are a-Changin'*, *Abbey Road*, *Summer Days (and Summer Nights!!)*, *Surrealistic Pillow*.

Dayna—tall, blond bangs, looking kind of corporate in her pea coat, scarf and boots—is already inside tidying up around the cash. She remembers her first record too: Elton John's "The Bitch Is Back"—a single in a cover showing the future Sir Elton in a big white boa—purchased in some long-forgotten mall chain store near her South Saskatoon home. "Every time we got our allowance we'd go there and buy a 45," she says. "We'd be some of the few girls in the store. Then we'd go back to my house—which was one of those places where the kids would congregate; anytime somebody had some troubles they'd stay there—and trade them around."

She's animated, effusive—the Type A yin to Stu's mellow yang. While her husband, humming, goes about his start-of-business duties, she tells me how her older sister turned her on to Cat Stevens, Jethro Tull, Lighthouse and all the other seventies stuff. How by high school she was big into Cheap Trick and, in the eternal question of Beatles versus Rolling Stones, always came down more on the side of the Fab Four than the World's Greatest Rock 'n' Roll Band.

The information tumbles from her as she sits atop the shop's glass display counter, kicking her long legs like a kid as she talks, raising her voice a bit to be heard over the sprightly Diana Ross floating from the sound system. Dayna freely admits that she is restless by nature: the kind of girl about whom teachers used to say with a sigh of exasperation, "If only she applied herself." Instead, she just wanted out of school, out of what then seemed like a provincial Prairie town. At fifteen she dreamed of moving to Los Angeles. Four years later she settled for following a sister to Toronto.

Now, back where she started, Dayna is fidgety for a reason. She's killed most of the morning picking up a total stranger— me—at the airport. The woman has places to be. Revenues at the Vinyl Diner have climbed every year except one since the place opened in 1996. Don't mistake this for the meteoric arc of a company in a growth industry. Along with putting in her hours at the shop, Dayna works for Canada Disc, an outfit that produces CDs and DVDs for companies and NGOs, and she's due there any minute. She likes the work and is good at it. It also has a decent benefits package.

That allows Stu to arrive at work in this blissful state. To run a business where his first daily task is to pay a single bill. He does so as a reminder: even though the worst shift at the record shop is better than the best day as an ad company exec—which is what he did for the first fifteen years of his working life—this is still a commercial enterprise. The lights have to stay on. Inventory has to be purchased. Merchandise must be moved.

Stu pulls out a yellow file folder that contains scraps of paper covered with the scribbled names of albums and CDs and the people who desire them. He shifts his old-school invoice pad on the display case next to the pink-and-white calculator he uses to figure out the 10 percent provincial and federal sales taxes that apply in the province of Saskatchewan. Working one-handed, he puts out a box of vintage soul 45s. Then he slaps some old Nick Lowe—one of Dayna's favourites—into the sound system and cranks the music a little. He takes a sip of chai from his blue Motown Museum mug. He works his neck around a couple of times like an athlete loosening up. "Good morning. The Vinyl Diner," he says when the phone rings. It is about 11:20. A happy man smiles a patient smile.

⌒

THE first record I bought, if memory serves, was a Booker T. and the MG's 45. I can't remember the B side, just the band's signature tune, "Time Is Tight," driven by Booker T. Jones's Hammond organ line. That I can summon up this fact forty-some years later, when I have long forgotten, for instance, the name of the first girl I kissed, says something about vinyl and me. Because it's a complicated relationship. There's a long gap in my listening memory bank until the Queen Elizabeth High basketball locker room and Kool and the Gang, The O'Jays, Harold Melvin and the Blue Notes, and Edwin Starr. Even then, I don't remember buying any records at all in the seventies when the hard-core music nuts my age were getting hooked on vinyl. Somehow, somewhere, cassettes started appearing in cars and crappy tape decks. During one memorable summer a couple of buddies and I drove around in a blue Pinto listening to an R and B mixed tape, imagining that we lived in South Philly instead of South End Halifax. But I recall not a single album being in the house that year, or the disco years to come.

One day in 1987 my wife and I walked into an audio shop near our Toronto apartment. I emerged an hour later in a state of shock, the owner of my first record player at the age of thirty-one. Life had surely changed. Whenever possible I made a beeline down what was said to be the longest street in the world to hit the gargantuan Sam the Record Man outlet a few minutes from the newspaper where I worked. (Friends liked to drop by our apartment during this period because it was the only place they knew of where the Dylan records wouldn't be all scratched up.) Millions of people visited that store from its opening in 1961 to its closing in 2007, six years after Sam Sniderman's chain of record stores went bankrupt. We'd walk in the main entrance on Yonge or slip past the outdoor chess tables on Gould Street. Then, pulse quickening, we'd try to figure out where in the place, which to the eye had no discernible pattern, to start.

Here, out of necessity, I developed the manual dexterity to delicately feather LPs forward with middle and index fingers at the right pace to make a considered decision to pull one out and stack it on top of the next row or simply to move on. Browsing, I discovered, was as much a state of mind as a physical act. Sometimes I actually had a goal in my head. Mostly I wandered around.

Once we all did. We were a nation of browsers and mean-derers. Price was part of it. Real prosperity didn't come to this country until the post–Second World War years. Our parents, like their parents, didn't part with a dollar unless they got 101 cents' worth of value. A commercial purchase in those days signalled the beginning of a long and meaningful relation-ship between owner and object. Discarded laptop computers, ice cream makers and video game consuls didn't spill onto the street from the curb on municipal clean-up day. People didn't just throw stuff away in the limited-choice age before the global economy and big-box stores because what precisely would be the point? Things got patched, repaired and, if need be, completely rebuilt. Only when the inevitable could no longer be avoided would a replacement be purchased.

If your family was comfortable enough that it didn't have to make a choice between new shoes or keeping the heat on, shopping was a blast. Families donned their best clothes. They piled into their fin-backed cars. They made a night of it back when shopping was still something a person did in person rather than pointing and clicking. They took their time, luxu-riating in the experience when department stores in Canadian cities seemed to represent the culmination of all of civilization until that point in time.

Who can blame them for being a little awed by the massive Simpson's in Toronto at Yonge and Queen, the colossal Woodward's at the corner of Hastings and Abbott Streets in Vancouver, the headquarters of the Hudson's Bay Company in Winnipeg. These weren't airport-hangar-sized boxes inside of which people in sweats pushed around shopping carts. The six-storey art deco building that Scottish entrepreneur

Robert Simpson built was designed by the same architect who did Toronto's iconic Bloor Viaduct. The massive stores that Hudson's Bay built in the 1930s in Calgary, Vancouver, Victoria and Winnipeg were fashioned in an "Edwardian classical" style. In 1930 T. Eaton and Company invited French designer Jacques Carlu to design interiors for its stores in Montreal and Toronto.

Those places demanded attention and commanded respect. I found the old floor plan for Simpson's flagship Toronto store, which in 1929 had expanded to nine floors. The lower level carried power tools, hardware, garden equipment and auto equipment, and had a coffee shop and lunch counter. along with a wig bar, a men's tailor, a smoke shop and a bakery shop. On the second floor you could get lingerie, luggage and ladies shoes, on the third furs, wigs and ladies hats. The fourth and fifth floors carried furniture and furnishings, the sixth was home to the bridal registry, the Elizabeth Arden Salon, and where a person got Wedgwood china, television sets and hearing aids. The seventh floor included an auditorium, the ninth a grill. The Arcadian Court, which occupied most of the eighth floor, is especially worth mentioning. When it opened in 1929—at the dawn of the Great Depression—the court could seat up to a thousand people on its main floor and mezzanine, making it, at the time, the largest department store restaurant in the world. The restaurant was soon said to be serving over a million meals a year. In 1962 the kitchen prided itself of being able to roast "six hundred birds . . . at one time."

PLACES like that, of course, were for the big-city slickers. Most of us lived in towns where it was a big deal to walk through the door of a KMart, Woolco, Kresge's, Zellers or some other discount chain, where instead of the Arcadian Court's fabled chicken pot pie we grazed on hot hamburger sandwiches washed down with soda fountain Cokes. In 1967, as millionaires inside the Simpson's at Yonge and Queen bid on British masters in Sotheby's first auction outside of Great Britain, kids like me were booting it down to the neighbourhood drugstore, where the new *Doctor Strange* cost a dime as long as you had a pop bottle worth two cents for trade-in.

The rack of comics had a handwritten sign exhorting customers to read after they bought. But management wasn't serious. We were allowed, maybe even expected, to take our time, because the tempo to life was slower before seven-day workweeks. Time unspooled at a more leisurely pace when a phone call or even a letter—not some device vibrating in your pocket—was the only way for people to get in touch with you. It was, admittedly, kind of boring back in those days before speed dating and spinning classes, when the ferrets and Arctic owls of *Hinterland Who's Who* were enough to command a Canadian's attention on the television. But there was room within the spaces when life was slower. You could think a little. Civility was honoured. Human interaction took place when there was no need to find some out-to-pasture type and station him at the entrance to a vast shopping emporium with the spirit-sapping title of "greeter."

It was that way in this country for a long time. Even, I recall, twenty-five years ago when I frequented the Sam the Record Man on Yonge Street in Toronto and they still respected your right to loiter. There, a quarter of century ago, it was entirely conceivable that a tall guy with brown hair and glasses could have said "excuse me" so I'd stop clogging an aisle. Being Canadian I would have stepped aside, or at least turned sideways. Then Stu Cousins could have slipped by.

At that point in Stu's life Sarnia was history. So was Sudbury's Laurentian University, where he knocked off a sports administration degree (baseball being almost as much of a passion as music). A stint in Ottawa working for—and Dayna still finds this hilarious—the Canadian Amateur Wrestling Association followed. It wasn't the right fit. "I applied for jobs at fifteen or twenty ad agencies—I don't know why," he says. In 1983 Stu moved to Toronto to work as an assistant media buyer, which he says meant "I bought air."

He bounced around from big-name firm to big-name firm. But his heart wasn't really in it. In the mid-1980s, as much as today, what he really loved was music. Not playing it, although he had taken a little piano as a kid. Listening to it. Had ever since he'd lain on his back in his room in Sarnia and tuned into Top 40 stuff on CKLW on his transistor radio. To be fair, a little escapism was perhaps recommended if you are the son of chemical factory workers growing up in a city where a job for life with Dow was about all a fella could ask for. Stu paid for his university by working summers in "Chemical Valley." He still remembers the summers of 1979–81 and the job he had breaking toxic, hardened aluminum chloride off the walls of a chemical facility. Afterward he would jump in his beater and crank Springsteen's *Darkness on the Edge of Town* up loud. Then he would drive around the southern Ontario back roads vowing to get the hell away from the life he feared awaited.

The adman's existence in Toronto at least let him scour the independent record stores he came to favour, like Driftwood and Vortex, and the Canadian chains including Sam's and A&A Records. He'd hit them at pretty much the same time I would, on the weekends and at lunch hour. "When I hated going back to work after lunch was when I realized I should do something about this," he says. He moved up the ad agency food chain. In 1991—"The Jays made the playoffs that year"—one of Dayna's co-workers introduced them. She invited Stu to a Smithereens concert. Sometime later they found themselves at a joint on Danforth Avenue. One thing led to another. Eventually they were up on the dance floor listening to a band cover "Alison," a song neither of them particularly liked, which happened to be written by an artist they both adored. "We talked about how much we loved Elvis Costello" is how Dayna, at the time a marketing and production coordinator with *Strategy* magazine remembers it, "and what a great thing it would be to own a record store."

The bond was cemented the first time Stu rode in her car. "I noticed she had cassette tapes of The Replacements' *Tim* and *Pleased to Meet Me*, which were big favourites of mine" is his recollection. Dayna moved in days later. The relationship survived an early musical crisis: Stu went away on a trip during a move and returned home to discover that Dayna had unpacked the record and CD collection that took up most of their new apartment. "I knew 'but they're not alphabetical' weren't the best first words out of my mouth the moment I said them," he recalls.

Cut to Vancouver, 1993: Dayna has snagged a magazine job. Stu is working fourteen-hour days as an ad agency supervisor.

Their plan to open a vinyl and CD store is evolving, just not quickly enough for a couple growing weary of the West Coast's mould. They thought about giving Calgary a shot. At some point Dayna said, what about her hometown? It made a kind of sense. Her parents were getting up there. What's more, in Saskatoon a nice house went for sixty thousand dollars, a pittance compared with the overheated British Columbia market. At the same time Saskatoon's indigenous music scene was lively, yet competition in the vinyl business scant.

Stu flew in one weekend alone so that Dayna's opinion wouldn't sway him. He walked around. He got the lay of the land. He liked what he saw. Six months later they had a house. A year after that they had rented a smallish space previously leased to an art gallery on a street just off Broadway. In the spring of 1996 the first customer walked into the Vinyl Diner. Neither Stu nor Dayna can remember the person and what was purchased. They just knew that at long last they were in business.

⌒

THE current incarnation of the Vinyl Diner is L-shaped and about thirty yards end to end. From any angle in the room you see greyish carpeting, a black ceiling festooned with rows of track lighting, and walls that are egg yolk yellow on the sides and a flat green on the ends. There's a small book section: mostly music bios, with some graphic novels and other stuff thrown in, and a stack of old music mags for fifty cents a pop. Mostly you see music—CDs and LPs, on the floor, on top of counters and chairs, in stacks and racks and bins and crates. It's a nice space: kind of drafty and a tad battered, yet with a clean smell that's devoid of the scent of burned coffee and sweat that you encounter in places that hipsters normally gather. A door leads into a storage room with a mini-fridge and microwave. Windows face Broadway. There's a leather sofa where customers sometimes chill, it being good business to let people sit down comfortably while they decide what, of whatever you are selling, they want to buy.

The shop's walls are papered with quotes: "I love the smell of records" (Neko Case); "Record stores are watering holes for dreamers" (Regina Spektor); "Hey, buddy, wanna buy a record"(Tom Waits). Plus more prosaic stuff: "Note: if you leave used records to sell and don't come back to settle up within 2 months, we consider them to be abandoned." The eye lands on a Funkadelic poster featuring a motorcycle and a bodacious Pam Grier aspirant in a leopard-skin dress. It skims across forlorn Lucinda Williams cover art; then, moving left, passes over a rectangular Hunter S. Thompson poster to settle on an advertisement for New Scotland Records, which makes the grandiose claim of being "untainted by scandal since 2008."

The building's musical lineage, by the shallow-rooted standards of Saskatoon, is long. Built in the 1920s, it was originally a jewellery store. In time a musical instrument shop moved in downstairs, which is now home to the independent outdoor equipment outlet that owns the building. By 1999, when Stu and Dayna moved in, the upstairs was occupied by an independent recording studio that later moved to a larger space. Being on the second floor wasn't ideal. On the flip side, Stu and Dayna needed some more space and a Broadway location raised the amount of walk-in traffic.

The footsteps seem to be coming from a long way off as the day's first customers trickle in: a portly fiftyish guy who announces that he is in search of old Black Sabbath, a youngster with a porkpie hat and soul patch who asks the proprietors about some band I've never heard of. The last strains of somebody doing a credible "Stand by Your Man" fade away. Between tunes the sounds of a place of business go on around us: the scrape of shoes on carpet, the hum of motor somewhere in the building, the grind of city traffic. Then some hip-hoppers called Gang Starr fill the air, urging us all to prepare to meet our moment of truth, which strikes me as sound advice.

Stu, by now, has been out to pick up the day's shipment of product, in this case forty records and eight CDs, from the usual distributor in Montreal, which he carried in under his right arm. He's done this and that. Now, in a short-sleeved checked shirt over a Vinyl Diner T-shirt, he starts punching in some numbers on the store's handset.

"Hey, Jim, it's Stu. I've got the new Bat for Lashes . . . thirty-four ninety-nine . . . Well, it's a double album." . . . "Hello, is Shawn there?" . . . "Is Mark there?" . . . "Hey, Scott, it's Stu at the Vinyl Diner. The new Swans has come in and you can come pick it up." . . . "Hey, Josh, it's the Vinyl Diner calling. Bonnie Prince Billy has come in and you can pick it up." . . . "Hey, Garnet, it's the Vinyl Diner calling. Yeah, hey, the Buddy Guy album *Skin Deep* came in and you can pick it up."

Stu speaks softly at about a hundred-words-a-minute pace. If customers don't pick it up their orders in two or three weeks, he calls again. If they haven't shown up in another two or three weeks, he puts the album out on the racks for sale—as per the warning on the wall. That happens, he says, about 4 percent of the time. It's such a low number because his people have true commitment. They have staying power. They may also live alone in their parents' basements.

Stu really has no idea how many of them—Saskatoon's vinyl-buying public—there are. He can, however, pinpoint the shop's primary demographic, ages fifteen to forty, and the secondary market, the crowd from forty to sixty-five. "Males outnumber females at least two to one when it comes to record buying," he says. I'm not remotely surprised. No one, at least based on my perfunctory research, is quite sure why. But the obsessive need to collect—whether beer cans, porn or Pez containers—simply seems stronger among males. Interestingly, he says, CDs are more evenly split between males and females, at least in their store." As a general rule, single people buy far more music than married folk do, and married folk who have eschewed the joys of parenthood buy more than those with kids. "When kids come along, priorities change. Sometimes after the kids grow up the parents become kids again."

I look around. At precisely 1:30 p.m. there are six customers in the shop, five of them guys. I could go ask them what their stories are. But I've had three hours' sleep in the past thirty-six. So I just sink into the sofa, as some kind of weird but enticing rendition of an old Stephen Foster minstrel tune imposes a narrative. I imagine the silver-maned guy with the down vest flipping one-handed through a bin, looking for a copy of *The Dark Side of the Moon* that will somehow revive memories of a girl, a summer night and a lime-green Ford Pinto cruising Main Street somewhere. It's entirely conceivable that the poppy-eyed fellow in the toque and leather jacket who took the stairs two at a time and headed with laser focus for the stacks at the back of the shop is a medical resident who just finished an ER shift in the province where medicare began. Eyes closed, earphones clamped to his head, he's sampling something on a turntable. Swaying, grooving, he likes, I imagine, British Wave. But what he loves in my little story is vinyl.

I've done my research. I know that LP sales, which peaked in this country in 1977, declined in the 1980s and then were virtually obliterated by the advent of CDs. (Which have since been replaced by MP3 players and digital downloads.) To put things in context, American record stores saw sales slump by 76 percent from 2000 to 2010, a period during which the number of record-selling establishments fell by 77 percent. We've no reason to think the trend in Canada is any different. More than ever, vinyl is for the aficionados, the artists who like to use actual musicians manipulating real-life instruments, the listeners who want something more than computer-generated sounds. In the long run, that may be its salvation. By the early 2010s, vinyl was experiencing a mini-revival thanks mainly to those young hipsters. To Stu and Dayna, it makes perfect sense.

Neither is a vinyl purist. They love their iPods and dig their CDs. It's just that they adore their vinyl records. "For starters, I like the size of them. Thirteen inches by thirteen inches is a much nicer size for looking at artwork and reading liner notes than five inches by five inches, which is what CDs are," Stu says. "Imagine if all books came in a CD size . . . that would suck!" Like Dayna, who "loves the crackle and pops vinyl makes and the warmer, less sterile, tones compared with

CDs," Stu believes that a properly pressed piece of vinyl in nice condition has a "warmth" or "presence" or something harder to pin down that makes it sound superior to a CD.

He even thinks the ritual of playing a record—removing it from the jacket, taking it out from the inner sleeve, raising it to the light for appraisal, brushing the dust off and flipping it at the end of a side—lends itself to a more involved listening experience. "There's a nostalgic feeling about playing vinyl," he says. "It has a warm and fuzzy association for me."

For Dayna too: "One of our favourite things to do when it is a cold winter night is to go through our vinyl, drink some wine and listen to one record that leads to a discussion about another. Pretty soon Stu and I are surrounded by vinyl, and it is three or four in the morning."

⌒

CUSTOMERS come and go. Stu knows most of them by name. A woman named Susan walks over to the cash, lugging some Joy Division along with other stuff. Stu writes up a receipt for $69.54. When a male with the patchy facial hair of an indie music lover quips, "How do you feel about losing your title"—a reference to the latest ratings in the city's alternative weekly for Best Vinyl Store—Stu laughs and says, "That will be $12.48." A well-dressed stranger comes in the door looking for help with the turntable she recently bought for her daughter. Luckily, the shop has two record players. So does Stu and Dayna's home. "It's always good to have a spare," he tells her. He fiddles around for a few minutes. Then there is sound.

Some people wave and head for the stacks. Others plop down on the couch, now that I've vacated it to talk music. Stu is happy to oblige. He can also gab knowledgeably about the Detroit Lions and the Toronto Blue Jays. ("The only way life could be better," he tells me at one point, "is if I owned a baseball team as well as a record shop.") He's fond of the graphic novels of Seth and Chester Brown. He admires the detective novels of George Pelecanos, who gets props for his ability to "get it totally right about music."

Conversation with him does tend to come back to that subject. Like any self-respecting music nerd, he's got his list of favourite artists—in order: The Replacements, Neil Young, Tom Waits, The Ramones and R.E.M.—and desert island discs: *Pleased to Meet Me* by The Replacements, Wilco's *Yankee Hotel Foxtrot*, *Some Girls* by the Stones, *Loaded* courtesy of The Velvet Underground and The Kinks' *Something Else*. (So, of course, does Dayna. The amount of crossover underscores how simpatico their tastes really are. Her most-wanted artists in order of preference are Elvis Costello, The Replacements, Talking Heads, The Ramones and Nick Lowe. The albums she could not do without are *Life's Rich Pageant* (R.E.M.), *Tim* (The Replacements), *London Calling* (The Clash), *Dear Catastrophe Waitress* (Belle and Sebastian), and *Get Happy* (Elvis Costello).

"Going to see Neil?" a young guy asks Stu. He and Dayna are. They go to see a lot of music, in Saskatoon and in more promising venues like Austin, Texas. The big touring acts. Also the locals they like to support by selling their discs on consignment and by giving them shelf space. While I'm lingering near the front, a smallish rocker in a hoodie enters. He's got what to me sounds like a crazy proposal: he wants to pre-sell his next CD to the Vinyl Diner and the smattering of other shops in the city. Then, when it's made, he'll hand-deliver it to them. By bicycle.

Stu listens patiently without a trace of judgment in his face or posture. After the guy has said his piece and left, Stu steps out from behind the cash to rearrange the stacks, flipping idly through the merchandise as he goes. There are dollar records and others for fifty cents each. He's got the usual categories— country, jazz, soul and rock 'n' roll, the clientele being primarily a rock 'n' roll crowd—and more esoteric fare like doo-wop. Spaces on the wall racks indicate pilferage. Occasionally Stu catches someone shoplifting. He doesn't call Saskatoon's finest. He just asks for the merchandise back and tells them not to bother coming back. "I fire them as a customer" is how he puts it. Then he returns to the front of the store and a stack of discs, which he keeps around for when things are a little quiet.

Stu reaches down, picks up an album—*George Thorogood and the Destroyers*—and pulls out the disc with his right hand. He looks at one side in search of nicks and scratches, flips it over and eyes the other. If everything looks okay, he puts it down on the glass. Stu picks up a plastic bottle of isopropyl mixed with sterile distilled water, gives a barely perceptible shake, then lays a little circle of liquid on the vinyl like a Michelin chef doling out raspberry coulis. He picks up a soft rag, wraps it around his hand and begins cleaning the surface in a gentle counter-clock-wise motion. Trouble spots receive particular attention. Then he flips it over and repeats the procedure on the other side.

When Stu is satisfied with the record, he holds it up to examine his handiwork. He spins it in his hands to consider the other side, blows off something, then flips it back for one last look. Stu lays the record down. He picks up the cover, opens it and slides the vinyl back in. He runs a hand over one side of the cover and then the other to ensure that everything is smooth inside. If the record is well enough preserved or widely enough sought, it goes in one of the cellophane sleeves he buys a thousand at a time. Then he affixes a sticker, on which he writes a price with a Sharpie.

"It's a formula," he says of the pricing. "An X markup, but I'd rather keep that to myself. The price depends upon how common the record is, how much demand there is for it and what kind of shape it's in." I ask him what best stands the test of time. "Led Zeppelin. They just transcend every new generation. I'm all out now, but once I get more they'll disappear as fast as I get them." Aerosmith "sells like Bieber." Neil Young and Leonard Cohen are also hard to keep in. Ditto Saskatoon's own Joni Mitchell ("If I get a copy of *Blue,* it will move right away.") and contemporary acts that could already be history as you read this.

Two women in their twenties appear. "You have the new Mumford and Sons?" The phone rings: a woman named Diane asking if the new Mother Mother has arrived. "Okay, I'll give you a call when it's in," Stu says, hanging up. A fidgety dude in a hunting jacket sticks his head in and asks if Stu is still buying records. "It depends," Stu says with a half smile. Encouraged, the guy hustles off. Stu knows enough not to get his hopes up. "People get rid of all their records because they're not into them anymore. They're broke or divorced. Or somebody is dead and there's an estate sale."

We've all seen those forlorn collections. "Trash, curb fruit, the bitter residue of yard sales," novelist Michael Chabon calls them. "Orphaned record libraries called out constantly to the partners from whatever fate had abandoned them." Stu collects lots of genres, so every disc calls out to him, promising something potentially great. He and Dayna scour the Internet and eBay. After work they go over to people's homes to look at old collections or they prowl defunct record shops to check out inventories.

Stu has bought collections of a thousand, even two thousand records. Once a guy showed up with a bag of records that Stu bought cheap. Among the dross was a copy of *Meet the Residents,* which, he tells me, was a parody of *Meet the Beatles!* by an avant-garde group called The Residents. Stu sold it on the Net for four hundred dollars, his biggest haul ever. Usually, though, the treasure hunting doesn't pan out that way. "I try to ask people quietly over the phone, do you have any Led Zeppelin, any Hendrix, any Stones. If they're from the eighties, any R.E.M., Clash or Joy Division. If they do, I'll know that there's probably some good stuff. If they say, 'I've got everything,' usually that means they've got nothing."

The guy returns, breathing rapidly from climbing the stairs, lays the first box on the floor with a *thunk* and says, "It's just been lying around the house. But I think there's some good stuff." I think I see Stu's shoulders sag a little at these words. However, the first few the guy pulls out—Waylon Jennings, ZZ Top, Nancy Sinatra—aren't a total writeoff, so Stu starts the appraising and inventorying.

Since this looks like real work, I stroll around and peruse the stacks. There's a pattern. Up front: the cool stuff like Son House, Uncle Tupelo, The White Stripes and The Miles Davis Quintet, along with the local heroes—the merchandise surest to appeal to the customers of a store like this. There's also rare material: the Rolling Stones' homage to the Ingmar Bergman movie *Through a Glass Darkly* in a cool die-cut album cover, the score to Alejandro Jodorowsky's crazy *El Topo*, the complete Jack Kerouac collection, the Beach Boys' *Smile* sessions.

The merchandise is predictably low on lame-ass pop. It's sweet to see some Gil Scott-Heron (*Midnight Band*) for $12.75 along with Canned Heat (*Cook Book*) and The Zombies (*Best Of*)—both for $15, which I guess makes them marginally more valuable than Jimmy Smith (*Paid in Full*) and Blues Magoos (*Psychedelic Lollipop*), both going for a penny less. The free market is clearly doing its thing, in my opinion, if no work by Elton John fetches more than $10, the Rolling Stones' *Tattoo You* goes for $4.25 and Jackson Browne's *Running on Empty* a mere $2.25. On the other hand, the Beatles' *Help!* is $30 and a fine copy of The Clash's big deal *London Calling* gets $31.99.

I wander around, rifling through racks until some piece of cover art, or a nifty phrase in a liner note stills, for a moment, my undiagnosed ADD. The most expensive piece of vinyl I find in my quick perusal is *South Saturn Delta* by Jimi Hendrix at $43.99. I am not fit to judge whether Dock Boggs's *When My Worldly Trails Are Over* is worth $22.99, *I Want to Hold Your Hand* by The Buggs deserves to fetch $20 or the untitled album by "America's Famous Song Stylists" The Diamonds is a steal at $30. But when I go in search of some of my favourite soul and R and B recordings—Curtis Mayfield's *Back to the World* for $18.99 and Marvin Gaye's *Let's Get It On* for three bucks less—the pricing seems dead-on.

Stu and his man settle up. Rockabilly courtesy of Wanda Jackson, who once apparently dated Elvis Presley but was now, incredibly, back on the comeback trail, fills the high corners of the room. Closing time looms. Dayna's on her way. The Vinyl Diner—which has had twelve paying customers, which Stu calls "a little slow for a Thursday"—is empty except for a tired man far from home, momentarily regretting his vocation, and a tall, unhurried guy who plainly does not. "Owning your own business means the work doesn't end when the door closes," Stu says. "This just happens to be work that I like. I never don't want to come in."

He says these words, with their stripped-down John Lee Hooker splendour, on an evening when it must be a hundred below zero outside, in this shop celebrating bygone glories, where the classic albums still live. He understands that the world of listening to music has forever changed, and that on this winter night many people who love a good tune will be hunkering down with their iTunes list. For all he knows, when I leave here, I will turn up my collar against the cold, put the ear buds attached to my MP3 player into my ears and disappear into the driving snow.

But Stu says retail is forever, and that there will always be a need for us to go and interact with a human being when buying the things that make life worth living. That may be just the opinion of a man who likes the look and heft of album covers and dreams of what they hold inside. It could be the wistful hope of a man who has found a way to spend his days doing exactly what he wants in the company of the things and the woman he loves. Sitting nearly horizontal on his sofa again, I really cannot say.

Yet I do know this: moments ago I held a cardboard sleeve in my hands. The dudes on the cover, lapels wide enough to land a Sea King helicopter, are *baaaaaaad*. Booker T. Jones and the MG's, crossing a tired-looking stretch of Memphis road in single file. The album, *McLemore Avenue*, is named after where their recording studio was located, in the same way that the Beatles named *Abbey Road* after EMI's address in London. I flipped it over and ran a finger down the back. It was, naturally, a bunch of instrumental Beatles covers. No sign anywhere of the tunes I bought for my best buddy at age twelve. He's dead now anyway. But I swore for a second I could see him. I could hear that Hammond organ build.

CHAPTER
FIVE

EVERY JESELLY ONE OF THEM

IT'S the bleak January of 2010, and in the town of Montague, Prince Edward Island, a middle-aged man wrapped in a blue sweater and sipping a medium Tim Hortons black coffee folds his long body into an office chair. Paul MacNeill's fingers dart across the keys of his MacBook Pro. After a burst of frenzied typing he pauses, thin wrists resting on his cluttered desk, broad Hebridean head angled toward the screen. He has things on his mind.

A day earlier the premier of this tiny province shuffled his Lilliputian cabinet, dumping the washouts, shifting the underperformers and axing a whole government department. Somehow the rest of Canada went on with life. In Prince Edward Island, though, the very ground tilted. The smallest province in Canada is also the most political. One anecdote, to me, illustrates this fact: in 2003, Hurricane Juan, a category 2 hurricane, swept through Prince Edward Island, leaving two-thirds of its households without power. The next day 83 percent of the province's eligible voters still managed to cast a ballot in the provincial election. Many of them did so by candlelight.

So yes, you could say that elections are serious business in a province when a couple of dozen votes here or there can swing an entire election. Politics does matter on an island where to the victors customarily go the good jobs, nice sinecures and other assorted spoils. And so—as he has done 670 or so times since 1997—the publisher of the weekly *Eastern Graphic* lifts his hands from his desk and types the introduction to his column:

Robert Vessey was barely sworn in as PEI's Minister of Tourism and Culture when he signaled he has no intention of making long needed changes to actually increase the level of service offered tourists to the Island.

As part of his new duties, Vessey was also handed responsibility for the PEI Liquor Commission, an under-achieving profit making centre. It generates approximately $20 million in annual profit, a figure that could be considerably higher with little effort. The problem is every Island government uses the commission as a patronage play land rather than maximizing its potential.

As an example, Commission Chairman Brooke MacMillan floated the idea of opening a liquor store in Cavendish.

It's a good idea. The majority of tourists travel there. Opening a liquor store in Cavendish is a no-brainer.

But PEI being PEI, we force tourists to travel 7 km to North Rustico to buy booze in an Island liquor store. We call that customer service. Tourists call it annoying. It's typical. Political considerations always trump common sense.

These are not the words of comfort. These are not the words of a man whose goal is to get along. Who knows what's good for him. Who knows how his proverbial bread is buttered. If a census taker showed up at the door of his comfortable aubergine bungalow in 2010, then Paul might describe himself as a widowed father of two preteens, a small-town businessman who wants to keep the girls in braces and ensure that the twenty people who work for him have bread on the table and a roof over their head. Technically that would be true. That just wasn't why I was here.

Winter on Prince Edward Island: I had been better organized in my day. Time just seemed to be of the essence. Magazines and newspapers were dying. Newsrooms merged, slimmed down, sometimes just vanished. Everywhere, on-the-ground reporting—the minutiae and intangible essence of a place and its people—was disappearing. "The news" was being replaced by the continuous loop of the Net, the mediocrity of the blogosphere and the conflicted windbags from the left and right that I heard on satellite radio as I drove over the Confederation Bridge from the New Brunswick mainland. "Real journalism" was something old-timers jawed about sitting by themselves over their soup in the seniors residence.

I know, I know: name an industry that isn't facing some life-or-death challenge in this digital age. Except this is my business. Work that seemed both worthy and assured when I graduated middle of the pack from journalism school at the University of King's College in 1981. Halifax back then was a vital enough news town to support two dailies and ensure that an aspirant kid reporter could land three decent job offers without leaving the city limits. Now there's only a single paper, the one where I work, which is one of the last two independent dailies in the entire country. Every journalism outlet I know of is scrambling, trying this and that, desperate to make sense of it all. In time a new order will undoubtedly take shape. Maybe Wikipedia and citizen journalism will write the first draft of history and become the caretaker of our collective memory. For now, this cannot be a good thing for any democracy. During the summer of 2009 I wrote some speeches for the man who would became premier of Nova Scotia. One morning I was putting the last-minute touches on a statement to be made at campaign headquarters. A couple of decades earlier—when I started covering provincial elections in this province—a campaign press conference would have been attended by some forty journalists who pored over every word the campaigner had to say. This time I hit send and peeked outside my door. Precisely one newspaper correspondent, a single TV reporter and a writer for an online outlet stood there. Après Google, it seemed, the void.

The demise of journalism hasn't been as stark in Prince Edward Island, where the entire press corps—some private radio stations, the CBC and two dailies, including the *Guardian* in Charlottetown, which boasts that it "covers the island like the dew"—isn't much changed over time. One day in 2010 I ran a thumb down the list of Atlantic Journalism Award winners. Of the roughly nine hundred different winners since the awards began in 1981, by my count around fifty came from Prince Edward Island. Paul MacNeill is on the list. He's won awards as the best community newspaper columnist in the country. He's also the most honoured editor in the fifty-seven-year history of the International Society of Weekly Newspaper Editors, from whom he's won a raft of awards for his opinion writing over competitors in the United States, Canada and the United Kingdom.

His dad, Jim, the founder of the *Eastern Graphic*, was also feted by the same organization, and is the only person to win both the Golden Quill for editorial writing and the Eugene Cervi Award for lifetime achievement in the same year. A little research also reveals this interesting fact: in 1987 the Michener Award for excellence in public service journalism in Canada, one of the industry's highest honours, went to CBC News and Southam News, which between them would have had a couple of million viewers and readers. The runner-up was the Montague *Eastern Graphic,* with a total readership of 5,989.

As an on-again, off-again reader for a couple of decades, I wasn't remotely surprised. I have always loved newspapers. But I adore community papers, most of them weeklies, which I devour wherever I travel. Who seriously can resist picking up a copy of the *Mile Zero News* or the *Oktotoks Western Wheel,* both from Alberta, the *Squamish Chief* or the *Gabriola Sounder*—published in British Columbia—Saskatchewan's *Watrous Manitou, World-Spectator* and *Prairie Post,* the *Bugle Observer* (Woodstock, New Brunswick) or the *Packet* (Clarenville, Newfoundland) or the *Northern Pen* (St. Anthony, Newfoundland). My home province not only has such inspi-rational-sounding publications as the *Light, Vanguard, Queen's*

County Advance and *Progress Enterprise,* but also a community paper called the *Casket,* along with the *Inverness Oran*—part of which, wonderfully, is written in Scottish Gaelic.

Reporters from the *Globe and Mail* and the CBC seldom go to off-the-beaten-track places like Saguenay, Estevan, Petrolia, Kamsack or Hay River unless a mine caves in, a fishing boat goes down or a vacationing cabinet minister strangles his mistress. Sure, these locales might warrant a dateline when politicians hit the campaign trail during elections. Sometimes stories magically appear when the weather turns nice and reporters from bigger places can expense their fly-fishing trip by filing a "colour" piece that fits some editor in Toronto's preconceptions about the quaint rural life. But let me let you in on a little secret: there's only one place to find out the truth about existence in those rural areas where most of us once lived: in the pages of a weekly paper like the *Eastern Graphic.*

Potato farmers, hardware store clerks and gas station owners spread the *Eastern Graphic* out on the counter and read it front to back. Seniors—pensions dwindling, options narrowing—push back the dishes and, with a snap, unfurl it at the dinner table. Bureaucrats in cramped Charlottetown offices lay down the paper with a sigh, knowing that the phone will soon ring and on the other end will be a politician all lathered up over something Paul has written.

To them a real newspaper printed with real ink by people who really care still matters. Paul—with his independent streak and his insistence on telling their one-of-a-kind stories—gives their ordinary lives meaning. In this Internet-dependent day and age, it is easy to forget that a Google search is not necessarily knowledge. That someone somewhere must draw straight from the source. And that the powers that be must always be held accountable. My question is, a century from now, who will the historians consult? Where will a person turn to learn what these towns, which once made up most of this country, were like? A blog? A tweet? A podcast? Or will they stand in the bowels of a library somewhere, wet an index finger on the tip of a tongue and begin to turn the pages of a paper like the *Eastern Graphic*? That's why I was here.

⌐⌐

BY 8:30 a.m. Paul MacNeill has been up for three hours. He's packed Erin, twelve, and Katie, nine, off to school. He's been to the gym. Now he's back home. He logs on, checks and sends some emails and peruses his usual websites. Then he throws on his dark Harry Rosen overcoat and yellow, grey and white scarf, locks up the house and gets into his new-looking Ford Explorer, black with a sunroof top. Paul is about six feet two, although the "MacNeill hunch" makes him look shorter, and lean enough, with surprisingly small hands. At forty-three he's got dark hair that's gone grey on the sides, alert eyes and a neatly trimmed goatee. With the height, the hair and the duds he exudes the kind of regal presence that wouldn't look out of place in a Starbucks lineup in any metropolitan centre. Except this is Montague—population 1,800—which means that he wheels into the Main Street Tim Hortons for his morning blast of caffeine.

Paul grew up a few blocks from here in the century-old house where his dad, Jim, and mom, Shirley, first began putting out the *Eastern Graphic*. People always said, "He's Jim's son—he'll work for the paper." Yet there was never pressure to join the family business. Growing up around ideas and in an environment that engaged the mind just rubbed off. After high school Paul enrolled in the journalism program at a local community college. His first job, working for his dad, was startlingly short-lived. "I'm not really sure of the specific issue," he recalls. "I'm guessing it had something to do with a younger son being a goof and a father calling him on it. Long story short is we ended up in the dark room yelling at each other. Whether he got 'You're fired' out before I said 'I quit' is a matter of historical debate. Suffice to say there was just cause."

Paul headed to the mainland, where he landed a job at a feisty weekly on the edge of Cape Breton Island, until the lure of better pay and bigger stories drew him to the Truro, Nova Scotia, bureau of Halifax's *Chronicle Herald*, the biggest daily in Atlantic Canada. His big break was one of those fluky things that tend to energize journalism careers. The *Herald*'s assignment desk was short of hands on May 9, 1992, when a fireball shot through the Westray coal mine, trapping twenty-six men underground. Paul grabbed a notebook, jumped in his Honda Accord and headed east. I met him for the first time at the disaster site—a tall, focused guy who seemed to know he finally had a story to ride. He didn't get home from Pictou County, Nova Scotia, until nine days later. But his coverage of the Westray disaster and its aftermath earned him a National Newspaper Award nomination.

Three years later he was back in Montague, a married father of one, working at the family paper. That was fortuitous: in 1998 Jim suffered a massive coronary while on the ferry from Nova Scotia after getting an honorary university degree. The kind of owner who flew by the seat of his pants, he had no succession plan. The finances were a joke. Paul, however, had cheque-signing authority. He was thirty-one. He may not have known it at the time, but he was already the person he would grow to be.

It is, therefore, worth noting that being editor of the *Eastern Graphic* holds little sway inside a Tim Hortons where old guys in tractor dealership hats carry on a conversation that has been going for decades and the girls behind the counter call everyone—the cleanly scrubbed folk in their Sunday best and the hungover-looking lads in the coveralls—"dear." Paul lines up like everyone else for his customary black coffee and bagel with cream cheese. "Hi, Jim," he says to a local worthy. "Scott" . . . "'Morning, Theresa" . . . "Helllooo, Smooth Guy" . . . "Good morning, Martin . . . Doug."

People bend his ear. They want to talk about the old photo in the latest edition of the *Eastern Graphic*. They ask about the cabinet shuffle. Someone wants the real scoop on the identity of the mysterious benefactor funding the area's new wellness centre. Paul doles out some gossip and info, but it's a two-way street. There's a watchfulness—that slight remoteness that all good reporters seem to have—that goes along with the easy Island way. "I don't know if I'd call the way I work a process as much as a way of life," he says. "I'm forever scanning the news, talking to folks. I don't really look for ideas. They just tend to naturally flow based on what I've read and who I've talked to. Tidbits fall into a column when appropriate. Could be weeks later, months later or more."

It isn't like working for the *Toronto Star*, writing a weeper about a homeless guy and knowing you'll never see him again in this lifetime. The subjects of *Eastern Graphic* stories button-hole Paul at receptions, in restaurants and coffee shops. The people he writes about have children who play with his kids. They're in the next foursome at the golf club. If Paul writes a column calling for the firing of the deputy minister of tourism, well, he just may run into her on the way to the washroom at the pub. If he sneaks into the visitors' gallery at the provincial legislature, the premier might just halt proceedings, point toward him and, voice dripping with sarcasm, welcome "the number one fan in the Robert Ghiz fan club."

Life here can be pretty claustrophobic. For all that, what a sweet little town Montague is. Located at the locus of three rivers and a nice, natural harbour, it was founded as a fishing and commercial centre in the early 1700s when Prince Edward Island was still the French-ruled Île-Saint-Jean. In the early days it suffered its share of odd misfortunes: a plague of field mice; a looting by a British warship on the way to the French stronghold of Louisbourg; near bankruptcy after the kidnapping of one of the town's commercial leaders by an American privateer.

Now Montague—with its great sunsets, its lazy Saturday-afternoon vibe, its "how-ya-doings" from complete strangers—seems, in many ways, in synch with the longings of the times. It oozes the ease and comfort that come from feeling anchored to a place and its people. It offers wide-open spaces when everyone else lives in cramped high-rises, and freedom from smog, crime and urban blight. There's also the kind of humanity missing in bigger centres, which comes from living in a place where people and community matter.

The question is plain: for how much longer? Anyone who

travels a bit in this country has seen lots of betwixt-and-between places like Montague. Its big industries, shipbuilding and fishing, on the wane. Its homes overwhelmingly populated by long-ago Scottish families. Its population getting older by the minute, as the young and ambitious leave for opportunities elsewhere.

Paul drives across the bridge over the Montague River. Past the old sandstone museum, the tanning salon, the real estate office, the restaurant, the small nest of government offices and the pub. Inside the post office, which is housed in a fifty-six-year-old brick building, he opens mailbox 790, pulls out a handful of envelopes, flyers and brochures and rifles through them. "Any day where there are more cheques than bills is a good day," he says. Paul gets back into the car. Four blocks east he takes a left, climbs an incline and pulls into the parking lot at the *Eastern Graphic* offices, which inhabit the second floor of a former fire hall, with the old fire truck bays below to prove it.

⌒

PAUL walks through an entrance that is without fanfare: a wooden sign, peeling green paint, a two-by-four seemingly holding the roof in place. Newsrooms, it has been my experience, are what we have instead of asylums. My first one—at a daily in Sydney, Nova Scotia—smelled of vile vending machine coffee and industrial cleaner. A few weeks into the job a colleague in the sports department turned on his tape recorder. Instead of an interview with a journeyman NHL player on summer vacation, we were treated to the unexpected sounds of the reporter and his girlfriend in flagrante. At my next paper in Halifax, typewriters flew out windows, angry desk men punched holes in the wall or, in a Captain Morgan haze, ran from across the room at a booze-up and head-butted the managing editor in the belly.

This newsroom is chilly and about the size of an elementary school classroom. It's early on a Wednesday, just hours after the week's paper went to bed. Everything has that postcoital feel common to all newsrooms after a deadline has miraculously again been met. Some twenty hours earlier Heather Moore, the paper's managing editor, sent the last story zipping electronically to a File Transfer Protocol site for download at an offset printing plant in an industrial park sixty kilometres away. Photographic images of the pages appeared on thin aluminum plates. The plates were mounted to the press. The inked images were transferred to a rubber roller that in turn printed the page on reams of newsprint winding through the press. Then, at some point in the early evening, the January 13, 2010, copy of the *Eastern Graphic*—"Bell Aliant meets with concerned Eastern Kings residents about high-speed internet," the banner headline screamed—came rolling off the press and into the waiting delivery vans.

At midnight, back in Montague, commercial flyers were stuffed inside the papers and address labels attached for mailing before drivers threw bundles of *Eastern Graphic*s into the backs of their cars. By now, the paper is on sale at grocery and corner stores. People are fishing coins out of their pockets at gas stations. Tourists on the ferry to the mainland are dipping their French fries in gravy, squinting into the morning light and scanning the front page.

Standing in the newsroom, with only a disembodied voice somewhere breaking the silence, I have no sense of the scramble that putting out a paper necessitates. The howler misspellings caught at the last minute. The mangled syntax discovered after the last story has already headed to the plant. Some years ago, Paul's father walked into the office just after a bundle of papers arrived and opened one. The front page carried a story about a land developer who had sold some land to the province for a nice profit. Unfortunately, that story occupied the same real estate as a story about a major drug bust in the area. Somehow, the headlines got mixed up. "SELLS LAND FOR MEGADRUGS" blared the sixty-point headline about the businessman.

Which was problematic: the developer, who was convinced that the *Eastern Graphic* was carrying on a personal vendetta against him, had already threatened the paper with legal action. Jim considered his options for precisely three seconds, then in his Scottish burr croaked, "Get every paper, every jeaselly one of them," and sprinted on bandy legs for the door.

Paul's door is adorned with two nameplates: the bottom one reads "Paul MacNeill, publisher," the title he's held since May 1998. The top one says "Jim MacNeill, editor and publisher." "Dad wanted out of Scotland," Paul says of his father, who was born in Castlebay, on the Isle of Barra in the Outer Hebrides. "He was a restive spirit who always wanted to see what was on the other side." I met the legendary James MacNeill once, in a Halifax coffee shop a night after he had been on a bit of a toot. So I have an inkling of what Paul means. Thicker of beard and body than his son, he told me how, after serving a stint in the Royal Navy, he landed in Toronto, where he met and married Shirley Nicholson, a Prince Edward Island girl. They planned to move to British Columbia to become missionaries, but the priest who recruited them died. Instead, they headed to Charlottetown, where Jim landed a job selling ads for the Summerside *Journal Pioneer*, half an hour away. Soon he had moved over to news because he was bringing in more stories than the people out there on the beat.

In time Jim was bitten by the newsman's fatal bug: the desire to own his own paper. "The early years in Montague were nip and tuck," he recalled. He worked seven days a week, selling ads and writing every word of copy that appeared in the paper. Shirley did virtually everything else. The paper was typeset in the back of their house. Then Jim would hop in his beater, take some of the papers to some stores, supermarkets and service stations and deliver the rest, door to door, by hand.

The *Eastern Graphic* survived two fires. Even worse were the ads cancelled by angry businesses and governments displeased with stories that appeared in the paper. "The people in power," he told me, "just weren't used to seeing themselves criticized in print." This was a new kind of journalism on an island where people seldom questioned authority. Until losing a court case, Jim printed in the paper the salaries of every provincial civil servant in the province. (They still run the federal salaries.) When a deal was struck to build the Confederation Bridge between Prince Edward Island and the mainland, he read every page in the agreement—a pile of documents several feet high—and harvested dozens of juicy stories about the deal. No one was immune: when Jim was convicted of drunk driving on the mainland, he didn't slink back into town; he ran the story under a banner headline on the front page of the *Eastern Graphic*.

He was larger than life, that's for sure. This craggy original with his love of peaty whiskey, the MacNeill kilt and a round of golf with one of his thirty or so pipes clamped between his teeth. This self-taught intellect so fond of quixotic quests—like trying to walk the coast of Prince Edward Island via pick-up-where-you-left-off spurts of a few hours or a few days. This lover of the underdog, so fond of bringing down-on-their-luck strangers home for dinner or standing them a round in the pub.

Sitting still was not a strength, his friend Denis Ryan told me. Ryan was a member of Sullivan's Gypsies, a precursor to Ryan's Fancy, the well-known Irish music group, when he first met MacNeill in 1970. During the sound check a guy nursing an Alpine at the Charlottetown bar walked over and asked where they were from. They hit it off. Libations were had. One of the band members had to be put to bed even before the concert began. Eventually Shirley called looking for Jim. At 11 p.m. he was found: he was on foot, halfway through the thirty-kilometre trek back to Montague.

Ryan moved to Montague in 1977 and ended up living there for three years. "On Tuesday night, after their deadline, I'd get the call around ten or eleven—'Are you up?'" Ryan, who now lives in Halifax, recalls. "I was in Lower Montague, which is four miles away. He'd pull into the driveway, and many's the time we'd stay up until daybreak, drinking our bottle of Scotch or just talking."

At the pub, or at a kitchen party, Jim listened as much as he talked. If he heard something that interested him—and everything really did—then he would jot it down on the index cards he always carried with him or in the several notebooks that were always going at once. Rick Maclean, who edited weeklies in New Brunswick before turning to academia, used to run into him at community newspaper journalism conventions. Organizers would labour to set up the best seminars and sessions they could. Maclean would just head to the bar and learn what real journalists do from Jim.

"You find out more talking to five fishermen than the minister of fisheries," James Joseph MacNeill used to say. Another one of his journalistic maxims: "Always have one fewer chair in the newsroom than you have reporters; it forces them to get out and meet people." Jim had other rules: "Talk to fifty people a day, not full-blown conversations, but a what's-going-on-chat. Get to know the secretaries in the government because they're the ones who really know what's going on." But these things too: "Engage the mind. Most of all, be the voice of those who are left behind."

⌒

"I'VE never tried to imitate him," Paul explained. "It would be foolish to even try. You can't try and imitate someone like that, because it just comes out false. At the end of the day we're just trying to live up to the spirit of what he created and to put out the best paper we can." Through half-closed blinds, the small office offers a view of Montague's waterfront. My eyes, though, are drawn to the wall and the yellowed front page from the 1963 first edition of the *Eastern Graphic*, then reputedly Canada's smallest newspaper. It carried what amounted to the paper's credo: "A weekly newspaper," said John P. Lewis, publisher of the weekly Franklin, New Hampshire, *Journal-Transcript*, must serve as a "unifying force to develop a sense of community. It needs to be a mirror that will throw extra light on the obscure and into the dark corners."

In walks a woman, petite with short strawberry blond hair. Heather Moore, the managing editor, has been running the newsroom almost as long as Paul has been alive. "Not a lot of fluff on her," he says of Heather. "She's 'get to the message, make it quick and get out of my way.'" One day, a few weeks before I arrived, Paul looked at his paper's website and noticed a small item about a house fire in Montague. The story, by the *Graphic*'s standards, was a little thin on detail. Paul sent off a snarky email to staff:

> Not sure who put the breaking news up. I appreciate the effort. However, simply saying that a house was extensively damaged by fire is not good enough for publication. Where is the house? Are there injuries? When was the fire? When will we update with pictures and content? What we don't know is as important as what we know. We need to get the basic information right. Until then can someone please take the breaking news sign down. I couldn't figure out how.
>
> Thanks, Paul

What he did not know was this: the log home in question was owned by his managing editor. Not only that, Moore, who is from nearby Murray River, had built the entire thing by hand. Nevertheless—and here is the astounding part—she still sat down as the flames licked at her possessions and hammered out a piece, on deadline, for her newspaper's website.

"I felt like shit afterward," Paul said, face pulled into a self-conscious grimace.

As well he should. This is no punch-in-at-nine-and-out-at-five place. When his father died, Paul met with the shocked staff a day or so later and assured them that the *Graphic* wasn't going anywhere. Their jobs were safe. They would figure everything out together, as best they could, as they went along.

Out in the newsroom sits a young guy with a ball hat on his head and ambition in his eye, hunched over a desktop near the back; one of those newshounds who won't be around long before moving on to some bigger marketplace.

Otherwise, the staff is made up of veterans, living by the adage that there is no age, only experience. Moore has been there for thirty-eight years. Sharon Riley, the stylish account executive, has been on the job twenty-five years. (When Paul's daughters were still young—his wife, Jeannie, died after coming down with septicema in 2003—Riley took Erin and Katie for the night so that he could stay in Charlottetown and host his CBC Radio call-in show.) Mary MacCormack, over in production, has punched the clock for the MacNeills for twenty years.

"Hughie been in yet?" Paul asks, dropping the *H* as some islanders do, so that the first name sounds like it starts with *U*.

"He's in after lunch," says Moore.

Paul makes a mental note to try to be around. Chunky, toque-wearing Hughie Graham, who has been associated with the paper, in one way or another, since its inception in 1963, is the paper's legman—the guy who knows everyone and everything in the district of King's County and is happy to pass on whatever he learns.

Paul's day, though, possesses a jittery rhythm; there's no telling precisely where he'll be when. As publisher, he mulls over the big-picture questions about corporate direction and might have to duck into an ad meeting to placate an angry advertiser. But he also directs the editorial policy of the *Eastern Graphic* and the three other publications in the Island Press stable. Normally he only gets involved in actually shaping the reporting or writing of big, or potentially litigious, stories. Yet Paul doesn't hesitate to show up at a news lineup meeting to share some scuttlebutt or to provide a little direction on whom to call in the Prince Edward Island government. Occasionally he'll tweak a headline. Sometimes he'll suggest a change to a lead on a front-page story.

The newspaper owner is a big dog in a small town. Today, per usual, Paul has lots of other stuff to do: find an emcee for the opening of the new wellness centre; round up a guest for his CBC open-line radio show. The phone rings. "Jesus, what about the rules he broke," he says, voice rising. "Yeah . . . Right . . . Of course . . . Yeah, honest to God . . . Who is the real guy who supported you on that . . . You're killing me . . . Oh Jesus Christ . . . Yeah . . . he still shouldn't have been appointed."

There's no way of knowing who is on the other end or why. Paul's job, at its essence, is to know things other people do not. So, in a voice honed from hundreds of hours on the radio, he talks to people; he reads documents, reports and press releases; he thinks and draws some conclusions. Many of them end up in his newspaper. "My columns generally connect the dots," he says. "You can't look at one government action in isolation of another. I spend my whole week reading and talking to people so that when I finally get down to writing I've already got a very good handle on the subject. The process is not tortured. It seems to flow naturally."

Having great material is 90 percent of journalistic success. Once, I would have wondered what there was to write about on this island of potato farmers and lobster fishermen. This province so small that its whole population would fit into a U2 concert and so reserved that Prohibition continued there until 1948. This island of weathered barns, white, tapered church steeples, sun-washed beaches and red soil. This place where within recent memory both the premier and finance minister at one point lived at home with their respective mothers. This land whose most famous citizen is a spunky orphan with freckles, sparkling green eyes and a mass of red hair, who never actually existed.

Then, one winter I found myself in Montague, at the southeastern end of the province. It's a long story. But it ends with me and a couple of strangers in a kitchen in a farmhouse in the woods. One of them poured a clear liquid into a mason jar. I took a small sip of shine. Though no mirror was available, I suspect that smoke shot out of my ears. At that moment I began to see things here differently. When you look closely, signs of an unruly spirit abound in this place where, in the 1860s, farmers launched an armed insurrection against the absentee British landlords who owned the island and the last rum-running vessel eluded the law until 1938. Even the population mix, though virtually every face is white, is not as bland as you might think: a smattering of old hippies and back-to-the-landers to give life some spice, enough descendants of Scottish and Irish immigrants to provide a Celtic rebelliousness.

As Paul talks on the phone, I leaf through a pile of old *Eastern Graphics*. The newspaper is a twenty-page broadsheet printed on thin paper. Colour on the front and back pages. Six columns. Immodest headlines—as big as fifty-five or sixty point for a real screamer—usually in Helvetica Black Condensed typeface. A huge hole for news. Newspapers make money two ways: by selling newspapers and selling advertisements. Most papers operate on a strict ad-to-copy ratio. The more ads they sell, the more stories they can run around the advertisements. About half of each edition of the *Eastern Graphic* is dedicated to editorial copy and photographs, compared with just 30 percent for most papers, which prefer that the lion's share of their publication be filled with income-spinning ads.

More surprising, to me, is what *isn't* on the page. No somnolence-inducing recitation of last night's town council meeting, as appears in many weeklies. No word-for-word reprinting of the latest missive from the local member of the legislative assembly trumpeting their government's "firm, unwavering commitment" to "the good people of X County." I recall Paul's response when I asked him about the *Eastern Graphic*'s approach to news: "It all goes back to the formula Dad created. He didn't want to follow the agenda of others, so he created his own. There are a ton of stories out there. We'll do the tough stuff and rattle chains, but people also know they can walk in the front door during fishing season and we'll take a picture of the big trout the grandkid just caught. There is no such thing as small story in a community newspaper. A warped vegetable is as important to us as a homicide."

And so, on the front page of the *Eastern Graphic* you might read a story about a sweetheart deal that allowed a school board member to run a private kindergarten inside a public school that was supposed to be closed and shuttered. You might see a piece about a Liberal riding association president being appointed by a Liberal government to the board of the provincial liquor commission despite—the *Eastern Graphic* discovered—having defrauded a previous government. There could be a piece about how an American artist received thousands of dollars in taxpayer money to sculpt a statue of Canada's first prime minister, John A. Macdonald, for display in Charlottetown, the birthplace of Confederation. Or one about how the province's provincial nominee program— meant to fast-track immigrants with skills for relocating to the immigrant-poor island—was fraught with all sorts of abuses.

This being Prince Edward Island, the front page is invariably full of politics. One of the best-known yarns about the *Eastern Graphic* harkens back a couple of decades to when the CBC aired a piece about the president of the Island's Liberal Party using his connections to get a government job for a woman who once worked at his law firm. The back room boy and his wife were at a reception when the story aired. He hopped in his car and drove down to the CBC studio, where he got in an animated conversation with a radio producer. One thing led to another. A punch was thrown. The police were called. The Grit pleaded guilty to assault.

Now, it's safe to say that a lobsterman from Souris in a similar fracas would have likely received a fine, probation and a black mark on his criminal record. Which is why Paul's dad grew so incensed when the judge who heard the case granted an unprecedented absolute discharge on the assault conviction. For the next year the right-hand corner of the *Eastern Graphic*'s front page dutifully carried an "assault case box score"—a running tally on the number of times that absolute discharges for assault convictions were granted on the island. Twelve months later the party president's was still the only one granted by a Prince Edward Island judge; every time islanders picked up the paper they were again reminded of the preferential treatment a big-shot lawyer with the right political connections receives in their province.

Glance at a few front pages and you can see how the *Eastern Graphic* ruffles feathers. Why ads are pulled in protest and phone calls are made by people used to getting their way. A few years back one of the highest-ranking deputy ministers in the provincial government cranked one too many at a Charlottetown restaurant. A newly elected female MLA was also there. What ensued was later described as "inappropriate advances" of "a sexual nature." Lots of people witnessed the incident. Paul, however, was the only journalist who started making phone calls.

Then one day his own phone rang: the premier's chief of staff and communications director wanted to make the thirty-minute drive from Charlottetown for a little chat. When they arrived, they talked about the deputy minister's drinking problem, and stressed the sensitivity of the situation. "I think they really wanted to look me in the eyes and see if I had the balls to publish the story," Paul recalls. When the next edition of the *Eastern Graphic* came out, it carried a front-page exclusive under the publisher's byline and began:

> The Ghiz government's most powerful deputy minister has taken an indefinite leave of absence after a female MLA complained he made inappropriate advances toward her.

Stories like that—a lone reporter unaffiliated with any media conglomerate staring down the powerful—make the rest of us journalists raise our glasses in moist-eyed admiration. When I asked around, I discovered such stories also give the *Eastern Graphic* the kind of at-home clout that's exceedingly hard to come by in a bigger place. The paper, according to Rick Maclean, who teaches journalism at Charlottetown's Holland College, challenges other island newsrooms to hold themselves to a higher standard. Pat Binns—the island's former premier and until late 2010 Canada's ambassador to Ireland—declared via email that the *Eastern Graphic* has always served "week in and week out as the province's Official Opposition."

Yet the paper isn't all "gotcha" reporting and stinging harangues on the editorial page. Flip to the Letters to the Editor and you'll learn what pisses people off—the removal of one of the wickets from in front of the Montague post office, unfinished street paving in Souris, the bugs in the community of Brudenell. Inside you might scan a piece about the guy who got into an argument with a woman, then, as she was driving away, kicked her bumper, causing $824.58 in damage. You might read about the facelift coming for St. Margaret's Cemetery, the ladybug infestation at Panmure Island beach and the winner of the province's Communities in Bloom contest. You'd read missives signed by folks named "Bunky," "Big Top," "The Grey Avenger" and "Fed Up to Here." (The *Eastern Graphic*, unlike most other papers, is willing to print pseudonyms just as long as they've verified who the writer is.)

In the pages of the *Eastern Graphic* you get a good sense of what people do with their free time: attend the Rollo Bay fiddle festival, visit the gathering of Clow Millar–Miller descendants at Murray Harbour north, play duplicate bridge in Souris, attend the 145th annual Highland games and Scottish festival in Lord Selkirk Provincial Park. Turn some more pages and you see pictures of the competitors for Miss Northumberland 2009 and a Taiwanese cyclist who recently biked through the community. You glimpse beaming kid soccer players and potatoes that look like the baby Jesus. You see the thoughtful faces of people on the street—"What do you think of the name change from CDP [Charlottetown Driving Park] to Red Shores Racetrack and Casino?"—and ancient black-and-white shots of sawmill workers, emblazoned with the query Who Are We?

Even the want ads illuminate. There you discover it is possible to buy a mussel declumper, a "female bunny rabbit lionhead" and a size ten three-quarter-length mink coat. You see exhortations to "get paid to shop," or for "cheap phone reconnect," a "debt consolidation program" and "discount timeshares." You learn that a two-bedroom duplex rents for $565 a month, and a "1977 mint, never-driven-in-winter Cadillac" sells for $7,500. You'd find that a lobster licence goes for a whopping $250,000, while a scallop licence garners a mere $20,000. You'd see jobs for blueberry rakers, aerospace techs, carpenters, farm labourers and short-order cooks. You'd learn that it has been ten years to the day since Artemas D. Macdonald passed away. And that Joe and Nora Macdonald invite you to an open house to celebrate their fortieth wedding anniversary from two to four at their home in Cardigan.

TO anyone used to the buzz of a twenty-four-hour news cycle obsessed with gore, sex and celebrity the paper reads like a dispatch from some whimsical place, where time stands stubbornly still. I asked Paul if that was how Montague looked to his father, Jim, when he arrived, filled with expectation, in 1963. The son wasn't quite sure. It was now lunchtime. Throughout the morning Paul had received six phone calls—receiver cradled between chin and right shoulder as he typed notes into his Mac—and made four. He thrice walked out into the newsroom to talk with Moore or somebody else. He had written a couple of lines of his column. Now, through the bumpy back roads of Montague we bounced, listening to CBC Radio, slaking our thirst with coffee sucked from plastic-lidded Tim Hortons cups.

Nothing had really changed since his father arrived. Except everything had. In his lifetime Paul had seen it happen: the old family businesses disappearing; the traditional industries waning; the necessities of life, like schools and decent health care, moving farther away. Anyone looking for a symbol of the quandary facing Canada's towns need only set the GPS for Montague. A few years ago Paul had one of the most frightening experiences of his professional life: at a newspaper conference David Foot, the demographer, spoke about the challenges facing rural Canada—and, by extension, the papers that serve them. The area he chose to illustrate the trend was Alberton, home of the *Graphic*'s sister paper, the *West Prince Graphic*.

Foot laid a chart of *West Prince*'s demographic makeup over one for Canada as a whole. They were moving in completely different directions. "There's a reason you're having a hard time recruiting nurses," he said. "There aren't as many young women." Foot showed that this once-thriving fishing and farming community was on an inexorable path: soon there would only be old people left. The most it could hope for, if nothing changed, was the second-rung status of a Charlottetown bedroom community. Otherwise, in time the last person will die, move into a nursing home or leave. Forests will reclaim the once-cleared land. Only abandoned farms and homesteads rotting in the damp will remain of their long-gone owner's dreams.

"The issue is do we matter?" Paul wonders. "Do rural communities matter?" It's a legitimate question that's being asked not just in Canada, but also everywhere in the civilized world. In principle everyone seems to like the "concept" of the rural life. Yet growth remains the goal of the moment, expansion the clarion call of the hour. Before the Second World War, just over half of Canadians lived in cities. By 2011, eight out of ten people lived in urban areas—with most of the growth occurring in endless suburbs and exurbs that materialize where farmland once rolled.

As we drive around Paul points out the collateral damage in the push for progress: the boarded-up houses, the now vacant sites where the family-owned store stood for generations. Between 2001 and 2006—when Canada's overall population rose by 5.4 percent—Montague shrunk by 7.4 percent. He knows big global economic forces are behind the exodus. He still blames governments in Ottawa and the provincial capital of Charlottetown for abandoning rural places like Montague. "The problem is government pays lip service. No real money. No real plan for immigration or repopulation. No real plan to change the economy."

A panicky businessman watching his market disappear before his very eyes? Rather than fearing Google and the other things supposedly killing journalism, he thinks publications like the *Eastern Graphic* are about to enter a golden age. "It's a period of transition that may take twenty years, but we will figure out a way to make money in this changing environment." In the meantime, revenues are up 4 percent from a year ago. Raises have kept pace with the cost of living. He hasn't had to lay off staff. Journalistic integrity hasn't been sacrificed to keep shareholders, or business partners, happy.

With his big hopes for his paper and his community Paul MacNeill may seem like a guy with his head in the clouds. A dreamer who, some might say, doesn't even realize his moment has forever passed. I see him differently: a guy who understands that a newspaper is more than a "profit centre." Who knows that Arthur Miller, the playwright, was right when he wrote that a good paper "is a nation talking to itself." Who grasps that when he tools around in his big-city ride with timeless river on one side of him and raw farmland on the other, he is bearing witness. When he sits down in his office, boots up his laptop and begins to type what he has seen and heard, he is not simply fulfilling the family legacy of comforting the weak and afflicting the powerful. By telling people's stories he is writing lives into being. Otherwise—with the kids gone and the grandkids not even bothering to visit anymore—someday soon only some gravestones in a forgotten cemetery might exist to mark the people of King's County's tread on this earth.

It is a lot of responsibility for one man to shoulder. And time is marching on. "I was always destined for the paper," he says. "But it's a big wide world out there and I'm not sure I can say the same for my girls."

That strikes me as a nice spin on a bad situation. I'm afraid that if my kids professed an interest in journalism, I might, in a weak moment, be tempted to put them in a room and lock the door until that thought went away. But happy, they say, is the man with purpose. If Paul can't survive, maybe all papers everywhere are doomed. What I'm trying to say is that Paul fights, for all of us against the silence. For this reason, wish him luck.

CHAPTER
SIX

IRON MAN

W ITH a glad heart Pierre Bedard stretches in the mid-morning heat in the Quebec countryside. Mint, parsley, tarragon and strawberry infuse the air. Hens and roosters cluck, quail and rabbits doze, a donkey brays, a dog—either Edgar, a mix of beagle and golden retriever, or King Arthur, a Cavalier King Charles spaniel—woofs. Pierre's rectangle of farmland is longer than Rue Saint-Denis, where he once lived in Montreal's Latin Quarter. Back then, the pinprick of home-sickness nestled beneath his breastbone, Pierre didn't think about how lucky he was to live in one of the continent's funk-iest neighbourhoods. He thought instead about the big mistake he had made by leaving his hometown of Rigaud, Quebec, at eighteen. Mostly he thought about how he had never taken to the big city. And about how much he missed the countryside's peace, clean air and quiet.

"Here is my ancestral land," he says with a vast gesture that takes in the tumbledown ski chateau in the hamlet of Sainte-Justine-de-Newton that he shares with his wife, Marie-Josée Lessard, as well as the animals, the woods, the hills and the delicate light. Pierre removes a semi-smoked, hand-rolled cigarette from his mouth, lights it and takes a deep pull. He's thirty-four, living in the shadow of one of the world's most cosmopolitan cities. To the eye, though, he reminds me of someone transported from a bygone age: he's got oval features, stout dark sideburns and eyebrows and a sportive half beard. Round granny glasses make his eyes look opaque. Though a thick tuft of hair peeks out of the top of his shirt, I have no idea what is hidden under the Afghan headgear, called a "pakoul"—kind of a cross between a welder's cap and a Shriner's fez—that his wife made him. He smells faintly of sweat. His hands—long fingers, cuticles caked with grime—have a pre-industrial nineteenth-century starkness. Pierre can't weigh more than 180 pounds, which, spread across six feet or so, makes him look quick more than dangerous. But his wide-shouldered leanness does not rule out power. Nor do those Popeye forearms, singed of any hair and corded with muscle.

Pierre worked until two this morning. ("When I go to the smithy and work, time stops—or at least slows down," he tells me.) So he's having a deservedly slow start to the day: sitting on an iron chair beside the herb garden, waiting for the sun to warm his joints, talking about his family's long history in the area. The son of a cashier in a restaurant and a lumberjack who also did some farming, he was a different kid: "I've always been interested in handmade things," he says in softly accented English. "I believed in that old saying, what is it, 'Idle hands are the devil's work tools.' I was always fixing things around the house. When I was young, I used to carve wood, making little lumberjacks and wood puppets. I had a flea circus and put boats in bottles."

They're good memories, you can tell. Pierre likes things that last. He treasures tradition. It feels good for him to make his home where his people have lived for generations. Just as he considers himself blessed to practise an art mentioned in the Book of Genesis; that was said to be practised by Vulcan, the blacksmith of the gods; that forged the scimitars of Saladin and the anchors of the *Nina*, *Pinta* and the *Santa Maria*. An art that, after all those millennia, remains as basic as ever: air, fire, water and metal—the power of the physical merged with the chemical. A man with a hammer trying, through pure will and muscle, to change the nature of a piece of iron.

As much as anything, it is the intent that matters to Pierre: what he does—forge things out of metal—is practical but, in this day and age of mass production, absolutely irrelevant. All that is really at stake is the tissue-thin difference between "a thing done well and a thing done ill," even as the rest of the world cares less and less about craftsmanship, dedication, patience and meticulous attention. "There is a right way of doing things," Pierre likes to say. The ecstasy he seeks isn't the thrill of heart-thumping excitement. It is the deep pleasure along the eternal road to mastery.

Pierre—who lives where he wants and generally does what he chooses according to his own schedule and rhythms—is a contented man, a blissful man. He doesn't hurry. His natural expression is a half smile. He laughs easily. Pierre stands, yawns, then walks toward a solid, beaten wooden building topped with an old weather vane. Some other laid-back soul would probably just stay outside and soak in the astounding day. Yet *le forgeron* lives for the flame of the forge, the clang of the hammer. Today Quebec's Brotherhood of Blacksmiths has dwindled to just fifty members. About half are hobbyists: guys with an anvil in the garage who dabble at forging. The rest are professional artisan blacksmiths like Pierre, who make and repair metal products—decorative, practical and sometimes both—with a few simple tools. That he is the only one who slavishly adheres to the "old ways" is as much hard-headed pragmatism as misty-eyed romanticism. "I am trying to keep the old techniques alive because they work," he says. "A house will burn down and the only thing salvageable will be ironwork. I'm doing the same thing the same way it's been done since the Iron Age—because it lasts."

Inside his workshop the air bulges with heat. Some kind of particulate stings the eyes. Coal overpowers the sinuses. What light there is comes from outside, or from the forge, which he started firing up a few hours ago. At first the eyes dart around, searching for something heavy, slow and nasty—a Minotaur maybe, over there in the corner. Once they grow accustomed to the smoke and gloom, it's possible to make out a room that's about the size of a small barn, which is what it once was. A horseshoe, symbolically, overhangs the entrance. If there is a floor, I can't see it. Two anvils—the smaller one atop an old tree stump—are visible. I glimpse a primordial workbench, a wooden barrel full of water—the slack tub, for cooling the hot metal—and a cast-iron block, called a "swage block," with holes and grooves for shaping metal.

To a visitor used to typing away on a laptop in a neat little room, the shop looks chaotic and tousled. A closer look shows that everything has its place: the pile of debris is scrap metal, which will always come in handy. The stacks of tools are different kinds of tongs, files and chisels and dozens upon dozens of punches. In a thigh-high rack I count twenty-six hammers, different sizes, shapes and materials, no two of them alike.

Pierre has four forges. A smith, I discover, can never really have too many. Before metal can be shaped, it has to be heated until it is as malleable as clay. Heat like that requires a safe fire-resistant structure to house the fire. Pierre's forge is wide based and waist high. The bowl-shaped fire pot has a hole in the bottom, through which air is piped to increase the flame's heat. A draft hood to draw off the smoke from the flame looms over the hearth.

Pierre shows me the drill: how he puts kindling and news-paper inside the fire pot. How he lights the kindling and uses a long, hooked tool called a "rake" to pile coal into the fire pot. The coal—shipped from Montreal in hundred-pound bags that cost thirty-five dollars each and last between a day and a week depending upon the work being done—is the bituminous variety. It has to be baked for a few minutes until the impurities are burned off. The dull-looking leftover residue, which is called "coke," burns more easily and hotter than coal. Pierre, who moves with an outfielder's unhurried grace, rakes away the coke that has burned to ash.

He pokes around in the fire pot for "clinkers," hunks of non-combustible impurities from the coal that dilute the quality of the flame. Once the pile in the fire pot burns grey, hard and porous he turns on the blower to feed the forge with more oxygen. Smiths used to depend upon a bellows operated by an apprentice. Pierre's blower is electric. He flicks a switch, hears the whoosh, then steps back and waits for the deep bed of coke to heat.

Today he is working on a *cadenas de cabane à sucre* or, in English, sugar shack lock—a lock for one of those small shacks dotting the Quebec woods where sap collected from sugar maple trees is boiled into maple sugar. Right now it's nothing more than a piece of wrought iron a couple of inches across. From those rude beginnings will emerge a nifty little conical device into which a heart-shaped key is inserted that sets or releases the shackle. Eventually the lock, which will take about sixteen hours to make, will retail on the Internet for three hundred dollars. He knows that's not great money. Pierre could make more dough cranking out in-demand antique reproductions for Home Depot and home furnishing outlets looking for a little old-style authenticity. He calls that "monkey work." And life is just too short.

Using a set of long, tapered tongs, he plunges the iron into the by now white-hot coals, then rakes some more coal overtop. It takes anywhere from 1,200 to 2,100 degrees Fahrenheit to heat a piece of iron to the point where it can be easily shaped.

Pierre doesn't own a thermometer. The shop's perpetual gloom allows him to read the metal. He knows that when a piece of metal is red-orange, he can bend it. When it turns yellow, he can punch a hole in it. When it is white, he can "upset the metal"—hammer the metal back into itself to increase the mass and make it shorter—which is what he wants to do now. Blacksmiths can do other things with a piece of metal, an anvil and hammer: they can "draw out" or lengthen the metal; they can punch decorative patterns into the metal.

When it glows white enough, Pierre uses tongs to extract the metal from the fire. Then he drops it onto the smooth surface of his anvil. At 129 pounds it's small by anvil standards—his other, a double-horned French anvil, weighs about two hundred pounds—but big enough for the job at hand. Pierre owns a homemade power hammer, which is easy on the joints but can't do the kind of precision, angled work he aims for. He almost always opts for muscle power.

By perusing the website for Kayne & Son, a North Carolina blacksmithing family who supply Pierre with many of his tools, I discover that lots of hammers are fit for forge work: bossing mallets, chasing and dinging hammers and French, German, Nordic and Czech hammers. There are hammers for planishing, polishing, raising and rounding. There are cross peens (with a wedge-shaped surface on one edge of the head) and ball peens (one end round and the other cylindrical). The biggest one I discover is a French sledge (17.6 pounds) and the smallest one may well be a doming hammer (.35 pounds), apparently used by armourers. Each of Pierre's hammers has a different handle to make it instantly identifiable. He lifts one that he forged himself out of the rack: two-foot wooden handle, steel cross peen head with a total weight of 3.5 pounds. Then he steps toward the anvil. It is time to pound some iron.

⌣

IN junior high school when I grew up, boys took a class called "industrial arts," where, theoretically, we learned how to make things with tools. My self-esteem suffered mightily in that class. I lacked the patience to measure twice and cut once. Nothing—not tie racks, footstools or jewellery boxes—was plumb, flush or smooth. Everything jiggled. When the shop teacher—an ex-navy diver with a chest like a bellows—started talking about fret saws and rip cuts, he might just as well have been speaking Phoenician.

That didn't stop me from seeing the value and virtue of such an activity. Perhaps it has something to do with a family tree that was dotted with electricians, carpenters, auto mechanics, bakers and Linotype operators. All I know is that since I started thinking about such things, I've felt nothing but wonder for the people who make the stuff of life. They build things, keep them running, then fix them when they break. They do something important and absolutely necessary—they may even do it with a little flair—with just a few tools and their own two hands. My admiration for people who work with their hands began as simply as that. But I also liked their no-nonsense ways. The sense of accomplishment of making or fixing something—instead of trying to anticipate the airy whims of some magazine editor—appealed to me. So did the notion of being rooted in the real world and making lives better in some concrete way.

Once we all worked with our hands. We know that from our names—Baker, Barber, Brewer, Carpenter, Chandler (a maker of candles), Collier (coal miner), Cooper, Draper, Drover (someone who drivers cattle or sheep to market), Fisher, Farmer, Mason, Miller, Plumber, Porter, Roper, Sawyer (a carpenter or one who saws), Smith, Stone, Tanner, Taylor, Tucker (a cleaner of clothes), Wainwright (wagon maker) or Weaver. With time, gigantic clanking, hissing machines would replace solo men pounding hammers in small workshops. In his book *The Craftsman* Richard Sennett argues that craftsmanship—which he describes as "an enduring, basic human impulse, the desire to do a job well for its own sake"—isn't disappearing. He thinks it has merely migrated. The Linux software operating system, for Sennett, is no less the work of a community of craftsmen than an ancient pot.

I fear we run in different circles. From where I sit there's an obvious de-skilling going on in places like Canada. When technology and the modern-day consumer marketplace can do so much, who the hell needs to make a wall that lasts, to re-sole Dad's hand-me-down brogues or to lift up the hood and see why the light in the dashboard stays on? To my mind, that's a woeful development. Some things can't be written down. Some skills—the understanding of the expert attained by a lifetime in proximity to his material, which is passed down from master to apprentice—disappear forever when the line is broken.

I pondered this last thought after reading a British study that pointed out that in some UK organizations, over 80 percent of manual workers exercised less skill in their jobs than they used driving to work. I've discovered no comparable figures about the de-skilling of Canada. But I do note that a century ago the province Pierre calls home had more carpenters (12,313 in all) than teachers, engineers, lawyers and accountants combined. In 1911, according to the Canadian census, Quebec had more stonemasons and cutters, plumbers and steamfitters than government bureaucrats. Overall, nearly half the Quebecers who held down jobs back then worked on farms. There were also more people working in the skilled building trades than in "commerce."

Quebec, at that point in time, had barbers and bootblacks (2,328), sextons (636), explosives makers (348), button makers (39), furriers (1,148) and white-wear makers (901). It had platers and polishers (138), printers and engravers (3,941), tanners and curriers (1,306), sail makers and riggers (15), along with telephone and telegraph linemen (987). It had people who made and repaired watches, clocks and jewellery (199), scales (38), boots and shoes (9,133), trunks (218) and musical instruments (373). Its citizens constructed fruit baskets and boxes (504), picture frames and showcases (62), brooms and brushes (293), bags and sacks (80), metal shelves (51) and surgical instruments (5). The great expansion of Quebec's heavy industries may have been just getting underway, but skilled workers were busy building locomotives (1,618) and toiling as machinists (5,205), iron founders (2,177) and metalworkers (1,060).

According to the 1911 census, a total of 4,812 Quebecers plied the trade of *forgeron*, or blacksmith. It's a lineage that goes back to prehistoric times when some short, shambling humanoid discovered that heating and smiting iron could turn it into something else. Smiths forged the weapons of conquest and the tools of civilization. As the great Christian cathedrals rose up through what would become Europe, smiths made hinges, gates and doorknockers, fences for cemeteries and clasps for vestments. In Asia they made plows for the poor. In colonial North America, where they made flintlocks and forged cooking utensils and tools, they touched every aspect of life.

In the early seventeenth century, King Louis XIV decreed that French artisans who had practised their trade overseas for more than six years would be allowed to set up shop as master craftsmen in Paris or any other city in the kingdom once they returned to the mother country. By so doing, Louis hoped to encourage his country's superlative craftsmen to immigrate to New France. What they did in this far-off colony, according to historian Robert Tremblay, depended upon where they set up shop: in Quebec seigneuries they fabricated hand tools and farm implements; in fortified cities and remote trading posts smiths spent more time making rifles, fusils and pieces of artillery. The ones who ended up in fishing villages made hooks, anchors and ironwork for boats.

In time, horseshoeing came to occupy of blacksmiths' hours as horses arrived for transportation and manual labour. Out of necessity, many blacksmiths eventually diversified. As well as shoeing horses, they made tools, nails and wheels. Occasionally they made a cart or carriage. Most of their time was spent making household items and the other objects of everyday life. They were, according to every chronicler of the time, more important than the village doctor.

～～

WHEN Pierre pounds metal, he leans forward at the waist. He grips the hammer halfway down the shaft. He hits the metal like a boxer throwing a short left hand or an angler trying to place a fly on the end of monofilament line in the middle of some moving water: with economic force—restraint rather than abandon. "The myth of the big muscular blacksmith is just a myth," he explains. "Most of us are small guys. Because it is not strength—it is technique. You don't muscle the iron. You try to be smart and let the fire do the work for you. "

Wrought iron has a grain that resembles wood fibre. That appeals to the woodworker in Pierre. You have to watch the iron react," he says. "You have to learn how to read the metal. You have to know what kind of a blow is necessary to upset the metal (really, really hard) or draw out the metal (heavy, straight down and square). You have to know how to grip the hammer: usually a couple of inches from the bottom with the thumb wrapped around the shaft, rather than over the top, which causes tennis elbow. And you have to know how to swing the hammer: mostly a flick of the wrist for light blows, but employing the shoulder and elbow for everything else.

Pierre adds, "Some people think you have to beat the hell out of it. Well, yeah and no. I prefer to use less force and go more slowly to making it a finished piece. When whacking the hell out of something, you lose some precision. If you go too hard, you will go past the point where you want it to be. Then there's not too much you can do about it."

It's work. Sometimes Pierre pounds a piece of metal hundreds of times before he's done. That's why ensuring the iron is hot enough is so important. Hitting a piece of cold metal with a hammer is about as useful and pleasant as walloping a steel girder with an aluminum baseball bat. By letting the heat do the work, Pierre gets a better result. He also gobbles fewer Tylenol. Even a 3.5-pound hammer gets heavy if you swing it a few hundred times. Sometimes a blacksmith needs a second to figure out what to do next. Pierre uses a little trick to get around both problems: he gently taps the anvil between blows.

That gives him a little breathing space without losing kinetic energy for the hammering process.

Pierre works on the sugar shack lock with a rhythm as regular as a metronome's: one, two, three, tap the anvil. One, two, three, tap the anvil. He didn't create that cadence. He inherited it. Pierre stops to wipe his brow. It is after eleven and warm. He's wearing tan, canvas bib overalls, a blue work shirt over a blue T-shirt, and brown workboots.

By the middle of the twentieth century, each Canadian rural village had three to five blacksmiths, or about one per hundred families. "Each smith had their own specialty," he says. "Some were more farriers who shoed horses. Others made sleds and did other things." The Sainte-Justine area, it turned out, had a good smith—Elias Seguin, a general blacksmith and wheelwright (a maker and repairer of wheels) who worked in nearby Sainte-Marthe during the early part of the twentieth century.

Picture a solid building with an ever-present plume of smoke exiting the chimney to his shop. Nearby, according to the research I consulted about how Seguin's operation likely looked, would be a small corral where customers could leave their horses while they waited for the animals to be shod. The entrance to the shop is wide enough to allow a horse, sometimes even a wagon, to pass through. The rear of the shop is gloomily lit, allowing Seguin to gauge the heat of the metal he is working. There'd be people, Quebec historian Jean-Claude Dupont concludes:

> The village smithy was always brimming with activity. It was a meeting place where men held their stag parties, learned to

drink, played power and parlour games and discussed politics. The blacksmith indulged in certain popular practices: he was called to re-establish order in the village; he struck the new fire of Holy Saturday in his forge and carried it into the church; he headed the labour group and maintained the fire used in flax crushing; his horses drew the hearse.

In rural Quebec in the early twentieth century, Dupont says, blacksmiths practised a "magico-religious medicine based on vaguely scientific notions, combined with folk beliefs and superstitions." They also acted as a sort of banker: lending money at interest and reselling grains, vegetables, meats and other produce that they received in payment for their services.

On a good day, a hard-working blacksmith like Seguin had time to shoe fifteen horses. But even in the early twentieth century he would have understood that his day was already passing. The automobile was the problem. When it arrived, many Canadian smiths headed west, where competition wasn't as fierce and, eventually, into the First World War munitions factories. Many of Quebec's country smiths transformed their old smithies into workshops for repairing automobiles and farm equipment. That didn't stop the trade's slow demise.

Pierre didn't give ironwork a second's thought when he was growing up in Rigaud. Or when he and a car full of cousins made for the big city. In Montreal he studied woodworking in a technical school—where he first discovered his affinity for old artisanal tools and techniques—and started working as a stained glass artist. Pierre was twenty-four and employed in a Montreal gardening store when he and Marie-Josée came to their senses and moved back home onto land sold to them by Pierre's papa. During the three-hour daily commutes he had lots of time to think about what he wanted to do with his life. At night at home he found himself going into the barn to look at the historic leaf forge he had inherited along with the property.

Sometime along the way—he's not sure precisely when—he got the urge to try to forge a piece of metal into something useful. There was no one around to show him the proper techniques, so he took out books from the Montreal Public Library. He went on the Internet. He scraped together some cash and went to demonstrations in Ontario and Quebec. Soon Pierre seemed to have two jobs: at the gardening store during the day, then at home at night and on the weekends, learning his craft. "There's a saying, *'C'est en forgeant qu'on devient forgeron,'* he explains. "It means being a smithy is how you become a blacksmith. That is how you learn. A book is good in theory. But there's nothing like doing it with a hammer and anvil."

Before long, he was selling his reproductions of eighteenth-century grilling forks, French potholders and double-turn locks on the Internet. Rich guys would hire Pierre to make cooking utensils for the hearths in their historic summer places. Railways came searching for ironwork. So did furniture makers—wanting locks for their cabinets and wrought-iron backs for their benches—and sculptors (one hired him to make a scale model of the Eiffel Tower). Historic re-enactors—accountants, car mechanics and ad executives looking to re-create the Battle of the Plains of Abraham right down to the scratchy wool underwear—contacted Pierre to make authentic pots, pans and tripods for cooking their food while "in the field."

Some people who do iron reproductions spend a lot of time with grinders and other tools, making them look as if they were made a couple of centuries ago. Pierre doesn't just make things that look old. He uses the same antique tools, mostly forged by his own hand. He uses techniques that, in essence, haven't changed from two centuries ago in rural Quebec. When he forges a rushlight—sort of a candle holder designed to hold a reed dipped in fat—by hand, using old tools and without an electric weld, it isn't just a reproduction of an eighteenth-century lighting device. It *is* an eighteenth-century lighting device.

When he heats a piece of wrought iron and hammers it into the precise shape of a nineteenth-century bootjack, you can almost see some seigneur, home from a day of abusing the peasantry, flopping down in a chair and, with a sneering expression, waiting for a servant to pull off his boots. Nothing makes Pierre prouder than when someone casts an eye over a piece of his and declares that it could have been made a century ago. "I don't just want it to look nice," he says, in many ways, over and over again in our conversations. "I want it to be right."

Once the metal for the sugar shack lock is the right thickness, he takes a prong-like metal tool called a "bending fork" and inserts it into the anvil's square "hardie hole." He lays the metal across one of the tines and starts to tap it with a small hammer until it starts to curve. When he's happy with the shape, Pierre writes a backward *P* and a backward *B*—his distinctive "touch mark." He rubs a wire brush along the lock to get rid of the flaws and to smooth and shine the surface. Then he takes a small yellow cake and starts rubbing it along the still-warm metal. If the metal is too hot, the beeswax will burst into flame. Otherwise, it smokes and carbonizes until it forms a black coating. Pierre walks out into the sunlight. He waves the iron in the air with the reverence of a Cree shaman performing the sweetgrass ceremony.

~

PIERRE doesn't need a lot of money, he tells me. "I'm not a greedy guy. If I have enough to pay the bills, then I'm happy. I could do more monkey jobs, making twenty pieces all the same, and sometimes I have to do that. But once I have enough money to live for a month, I do the stuff I want to do. It is the kick of making something unique. I want to be proud of what I've done. I would rather please myself than please the customer. Real blacksmiths are not forging for our customers. We are forging for other blacksmiths."

Inside his house the self-taught chef drops pasta into the boiling water and turns up the heat under the homemade tomato sauce. He breaks the hard Quebec cheese into hunks and serves up bread, still warm from the bread maker. The meal is comfort in a bowl. I shouldn't be surprised. Pierre has an unusual bag of hobbies—cooking, playing the sitar, crafting the kind of handmade wooden toys with moving parts popular at the start of the twentieth century—and seems competent at all of them. I ask him how long it takes to become a good blacksmith. He ponders that for a second before saying that the answer depends on the style and complexity of the work. Then he adds, "Being a blacksmith is like cooking. Once you really know the recipe—once you understand every ingredient, why it's there and how it must be treated—then you can throw it away and go by taste."

Pierre isn't measuring himself against the stuff you see at the local store. He has a higher standard: his Quebec predecessors, the purveyors of his favourite artistic styles, Italian art nouveau and early-American Pennsylvania Dutch. Mostly he wants to earn the esteem of his mentor, Lloyd Johnston, whose people have been blacksmithing in the Kawartha Lakes area of Ontario since 1831. At seventeen Lloyd told his father that he was never going to work where he got his hands dirty. Nonetheless, he studied engineering at university, graduated and then went looking for something to do with his hands "for a while." Now he and Pierre talk once a week on the phone, and meet at old-time craft festivals. Every month or so Pierre hops in his pickup and makes the six-hour drive to Woodville, Ontario, where Lloyd, one of the province's thirty-or-so professional blacksmiths lives and operates his blacksmithing school.

Guys like this have to stick together. Blacksmithing is a lonely business and Pierre a social guy. This afternoon he is forging a long-handled frying pan for some history buffs looking to re-create the days of the coureurs de bois. Some jobs require more than two hands. Fortunately, today he has help. A man about Pierre's age has shown up. His face is angular; his eyes are dark and Gallic, the bequests of ancestors who made the long Atlantic crossing from France. He is marginally taller than Pierre is, lanky, with a ponytail and a dark beard. He wears a loose-fitting denim shirt, work pants and boots. He carries a plastic forty-ounce bottle of Coke.

Though Dominique Marleau lives in Montreal, he was born in Rigaud, the same as Pierre. One day in 2006 he was wandering around at a traditional arts festival in a town called Vaudreuil, when he discovered Pierre putting on a blacksmithing demonstration. "I said, 'Wow, that is neat,'" explains Dominique. "I'm a train conductor by day so I like things made of iron. But I also like the fire and doing things the old way. I like being able to re-create the way something was made three hundred years ago."

Blacksmiths used to have full-time assistants who operated the bellows, stirred the fire and carried the coals. Pierre would dearly love to have an apprentice to whom he could pass on the time-honoured techniques. In time, maybe Dominique will live up to his promise to move home and really get serious about learning the craft. For now the best he can do is a once-a-week jaunt to Sainte-Justine-de-Newton to absorb what Pierre can show him.

By the time Dominique arrives Pierre has already prepared the forge—cleaning the fire pot, lighting the newspaper, piling the coal atop the coke, adding some kindling, turning on the air. The customer for the long-handled frying pan isn't paying enough to forge the whole thing from scratch. So Pierre takes an old frying pan and cuts the handle off with a grinder. To connect the pan to the handle, he needs a short, T-shaped chunk of metal. Pierre marks one end of the metal with a piece of chalk and then shoves it into the coals. When the metal is yellow-hot, he lifts it onto the anvil and hits it with the hammer, sending flecks of scale that formed on the hot iron flying into the air seemingly at the speed of sound. "Blacksmiths get burned a lot," he says. "If something falls, the natural reflex is to catch it. I used to try and pluck those chips. You have to lose the reflex of catching them."

Pierre rummages around in a pile of metal for a piece of flat bar. The one he chooses is eight feet long and five-sixteenths of an inch thick. When it's hot enough, he nods to Dominique, who has been patiently watching, his hand absentmindedly on the handle of the cross peen beam sledgehammer by his side. It is nearly 4 p.m. They are ready to forge the iron. Pierre smacks the metal with his ball peen hammer. Dominique smacks it with his sledge. Then they're off, Pierre leading the way, Dominique following a beat later.

Usually the blacksmith's helper is supposed to strike the iron in the middle. When Pierre wants that to change, he indicates where the sledge blows are to fall by touching the spot with his hand hammer. If Pierre gives the anvil quick, light blows, it is a signal for Dominique to strike quicker by putting more of his lanky body behind each blow. When Pierre wants him to pound harder, he hits the metal with more force with his ball peen hammer. If he wants Dominique to strike more softly, he lowers the intensity of his own blows. As they proceed, Pierre sometimes uses verbal cues—"Yep, yep, yep" or "Go, go, go" or "Harder, harder, harder"—to get the desired effect. When Pierre places the head of his hammer on the anvil, Dominique strikes the metal one last time.

They scarf the end of the handle and the edge of the T-shaped piece. They pound them down so that they make a clean weld. Pierre takes a wire brush to the metal to scrape away the scales and then adds borax, a white flux that prevents oxidization, to the two pieces of metal about to be bound. The metal goes back in the coals. The two pieces are placed on the anvil, one over the other, scarf upon scarf, forming an orange cross. They start hammering the metal in the centre of the weld, pushing everything out to the edges. On and on they pound. They pound the metal until the molecules are so full of energy that they jump from one piece of metal to the other. Only then does Pierre lay his hammer down.

While the handle reheats, Pierre pokes around in the shop some more. He returns with a punch. He pops a trio of holes in the T-shaped handle end and pushes a homemade rivet—three-sixteenths of an inch long with a mushroom cap head—into each hole. Once the rivets are in place he picks up a half-pound ball peen hammer and pounds the rivets down. When they're flush, he hits each head four times with the hammer to make a diamond shape.

Dominique lets out a "whoo-hoo." They mumble some words in French that I can't quite catch. But I get the drift. It is the spring of 2010. And yet here stand these two, in this time where everything is written in sand and immortality is a tune by Pearl Jam. Pierre and Dominique had to know that there was nothing really at stake today other than doing something well for its own sake. For them that's enough. So I gaze at this scene—the gloom, smoke and sparks, the elemental tools, the happy men doing work that hasn't changed in essence since the Iron Age—and try to commit it to memory. They make things to last at a time when everything is obliterated by the click of a mouse and the next thing to roll off the assembly line. The least I can do is bear witness. While someone still can.

CHAPTER
SEVEN

READING THE GRASS

ONE November morning I got up and got in my rental car in Hanna, the Alberta town closest to Marj Venot's place. I exited the parking lot where the young guys leave their bull-barred, rocker-panelled pickups running while they have a couple of pops in the bar by the motel. I drove past their parents' homes: a generation or two back the original Scots, German-Russians and Americans who settled the area. Beyond a new fire hall, a prosperous seniors residence, ball fields sponsored by the Kinsmen and tennis courts covered in early winter snow I discovered Hanna just stops. Then the horizon opens in a way that makes a city boy from a place where everything is crabbed together take a series of deep breaths.

I lived in Calgary for a couple of years in the late eighties, when the province was in one of those oil-price-related slumps that would pass for prosperity most anywhere else in this country. We hit the highway to Banff and Lake Louise. We went to barbecues in the foothills of the Rockies. Once we drove as far as the Badlands—about forty-five minutes from Hanna—to see a place where dinosaurs had roamed. I'm not sure why, but we never made it to the short-grass country. So I'm quite unprepared for the roll of the flatlands, the scale of the sky, the tapering highway that just goes and goes. I drove up the night before, in fog as thick as I've encountered on Newfoundland's Great Northern Peninsula. Now it has burned off, leaving a savannah so stunningly empty that it makes me scan the vista for a tree or animal so I could get my bearings.

When we spoke over the phone, Marj told me to watch out for the stop sign or I'd miss the road to her place. She might have been just screwing with the city boy. Heading east along Solon Road, there's only one stop sign. It can be seen from a couple of miles away. I flip my blinker on for the right turn. I realized, the moment I did so, that this was stupid: over the ten-mile stretch to Veno Ranches I see a total of three man-made structures. I don't pass one car. I don't see a single human being. Marj's property sits on the uppermost edge of Alberta's Special Areas, a five-million-acre extension of the Great Plains grasslands that run from the Missouri River to the Rocky Mountains. It is land that, in Marj's words, "has not had man messing with it." Last time someone bothered to count, five thousand people lived in the Special Areas, which works out to one person per thousand acres of land.

The cow-per-acre ratio on her land is much higher. The woman who owns them does not give them names like Minnie, Dollie or Bessie. Marj, who when I arrive is shooing away Duke, her oldest herd dog, doesn't need to. In her mind she says, "There's the one with the short tail" or "Here comes the scared one" or "There goes the rust-coloured one." A few of the bulls, it is true, have nicknames like "Hustler" and "Grid Iron." A lot of the cattle can only be told apart by the number on the ear tag: 249, 5440, 47 and so on. Often she refers to them, respectfully, as the "old girls"—although, if need be, she will call them anything necessary to get them to move along.

It helps that cattle don't roam far, even on lands as expansive as these are. Marj and her husband, Murray McArthur, have 19.5 sections of land between the two of them. A section is 640 acres. So their trio of ranches contains 12,480 acres of Alberta ranch land. On it they raise three hundred purebred Angus cows for "seed stock" and another three hundred head of commercial Angus cattle for beef. "More than the average," Marj says of her ranch, "but there're ones that are bigger." Particularly these days, when so many ranchers want out and those who stay have to grow to survive. Even so, it's big enough that Murray is off today in the Cessna 150 two-seater airplane they bought to better keep an eye on their land and herd.

Marj, who talks in miles rather than kilometres, is old school. When the weather is nice, she gets on her saddle horse at first light. Then she and Duke just ride out into the land. Many days when she returns home after a day of mending fences, checking her herd and making sure the deer hunters haven't left her gates open, it will be dark. Usually she won't have seen a single human being since departing in the morning. She does not necessarily see this as a problem.

Marj is fifty-six the day I arrive. A squarely built woman with a no-fuss haircut. Neither her temperament nor her appearance suggests a humanity-hating hermit. She brings to mind Bob Dylan's line to an interviewer about being "Exclusive, maybe, but not reclusive." Marj's green eyes are level behind wire-rimmed glasses. But her face—undamaged by the elements despite all those days outside—erupts when she laughs, which is often, and a little surprising. For Marj has seen her share of troubles. She has had moments that have made her wonder if there is anything resembling fairness on this old earth. She has stood there with no place to go but forward. Then she has put one foot squarely in front of the other until she is as I find her here today: a woman who has made her way in a man's world, a third-generation Alberta rancher at a time when a host of difficulties—mad cow, the Canadian dollar, surging feed prices and the developed world's desire to eat less beef—are making cattle ranchers an endangered species.

That she doesn't make too big a deal of everything she's had to bear could be because that's just not done in a place whose story, on the Town of Hanna website, begins this way:

History is not a term which affixes itself easily to community life which is so much a part of each one of us. In Hanna, and other small communities, we are familiar with the events, the families and the culture which is an intimate part of everyday living. Nevertheless, 85 years of relentless effort under every form of adversity . . . drought, hail, blizzards, floods, rust, smut, poverty . . . qualifies as history.

Her people's story fits the mould. It really begins in 1909, when her grandfather Hugh Nester took his blacksmith's forge from an Ontario village called Tara to an Alberta hamlet named Bassano, where there were horses to be shod and land for a man with ambition in his heart. "He built a shack and broke ten acres" is how Marj puts it. "He did what he had to do and married the girl from across the road."

She was a Holcomb from North Dakota. Evelyn Holcomb's people may have seen one of the posters advertising "The Last Best West" or "the flour barrel of the world," a country offering "homes for millions" and "free land." They may have even sat gape-mouthed in some prairie hall or auditorium listening to an agent hired by the Canadian government— hell-bent on populating the West now that wheat sales were booming and a bout of railway building was underway—who was paid a commission for every man woman and child he persuaded to settle in western Canada.

The great arc of history had pretty much emptied out the place where the Holcombs ended up: by the 1890s, buffalo hunters had killed off the large herds of bison that had once roamed southern Alberta and Saskatchewan. Starving and marginalized, the Bloods, Cree and Siksikas limped onto reserves. As the North West Mounted Police marched west, ranchers—many of them from the United States, where the frontier had been closed off—moved into the prairies and foothills. For a while a powerful compact of ranchers kept the homesteaders at bay. But, desirous of open settlement, Ottawa had its mind made up. The winter of 1906–07 helped things along: those same ranchers saw at least half of their herds starve to death in the bitter cold. The ranchers went bankrupt, or they just up and left. In 1908 Ottawa amended the Dominion Lands Act, giving a quarter section of free land to newly arriving immigrants, opening twenty-eight million acres in southern Saskatchewan and Alberta.

Though many homesteaders, like Hugh Nester, came from eastern Canada, the government pitchmen really wanted immigrants from Europe and the United Kingdom. Clifford Sifton, the Canadian minister of the interior, saw midwestern American farmers as the perfect recruits: they knew how to farm the prairie soil. Mostly they spoke the same language and shared the same values as their counterparts in western Canada. They were also desperate: the good American land was gone. In 1890 the American West was officially closed. Though the numbers were unreliable, between 1896 and 1910, it is estimated that close to six hundred thousand Americans poured into the Canadian West in search of cheap land.

"Grandma's people ended up in a dry, arid place called the Palliser Triangle," Marj tells me. We're in her living room, looking at old photos of her predecessors. The frontier where they landed was so called because a British aristocrat named John Palliser had passed through there in 1857–58 and declared the area "desert, or semi-desert in character, which can never be expected to become occupied by settlers." Other later visitors felt much the same way. Colonel G.A. French, who led the North West Mounted Police's great trek west in 1874, noted he had expected, for some reason, to encounter a "luxuriant pasture, according to most accounts, a veritable Garden of Eden." Instead, he found "for at least sixty to seventy miles in each direction . . . little better than a desert, not a tree to be seen anywhere, ground parched and poor."

It rarely rained there. The thin topsoil compounded the problems. The winds out of the Rockies came "soughing across the land, howling through the fences and telegraph lines, aligning small coulees," in the words of historian David Jones, "lifting the typical thin brown regional soils and piling vast sand dunes." In the Badlands around present-day Drumheller the winds cleaved away all vegetation and carved out strange formations called "hoodoos." Everywhere, Jones wrote, the blowing was all-powerful. "It was as if King Aeolus, ruler of the winds, had hatched a foul plot high in the Rockies and had set the west wind and the south wind, those normally gentle and compliant breezes, against each other in a struggle of influence and dominion."

Newcomers like the Nesters and Holcombs, knowing nothing about this, came anyway. Idyllic images of free land and bountiful harvests danced in their heads. "Southern Alberta," gushed a writer for the *Canada West* magazine, was "a land blessed of the Gods—a land over which bending nature never smiles and into whose cradle she emptied her golden horn." Before the influx, southeastern Alberta was home to around nine thousand residents. Within ten years, the region's settler population increased eightfold. Almost all of them lived on new farms where wheat was the principal crop.

᠆᠆

EVELYN Nester was about Marj's height, five foot two. Back in Carrington, North Dakota, she played the piano for silent movies and in a dance band. Life in a prairie farm town would have prepared her for the drought that hit the Prairies

soon after her marriage. But perhaps not for the successive years of rainlessness and crop failure that followed right
through the 1930s.

Yet they hung in. They endured, even as their lands
became the prairie dust bowl of history and the very symbol
of the Dirty Thirties. Even when Evelyn, in Marj's words,
discovered that Hugh was "quite dead one morning" in 1933.
Picture, if you would, her predicament: in midst of the Great
Depression, living on a prairie farm that, after a decade of
drought and every other kind of misfortune, must have seemed
godforsaken. Did I forget to mention that she had seven children ranging in age from twelve years to eighteen months?

Marj's dad and aunts and uncles would tell how Evelyn
played the piano at country dances for a few dollars, then
ride home alone on horseback or in a buggy across the empty
Alberta landscape to face her brood and more hard work. They
mentioned how her fingers bled from playing so long and
always being so cold. And how, while Marj's dad and his older
brother looked after the livestock, she sold homemade butter
and bread to neighbouring bachelors to scratch out a living for
the household.

"They talked about her sense of humour," recalls Marj,
"her ability to make a meal out of most anything that was
available and her determination to keep them all in school as
long as possible so they could make something of themselves."
Evelyn Nester died old before her time, when a brain tumour
took her at age fifty-three. Marj wasn't born until six years
later, so her memories of her grandma are second-hand. But,
she says, "I've often thought of her and what she endured with
seven kids, no running water or indoor plumbing, no vehicle

or any of the other modern conveniences that we have now."

Marj thought about her grandma a lot after her first husband, Greg Veno, died in 1991 following a long, spirit-sapping fight with cancer. The parallels were cruel: Marj owed the bank half a million dollars. She had 2,500 acres of cultivated land to work and a herd of two hundred commercial cows to raise. She was a single mother of a fourteen-year-old daughter, left to her own designs in a land where life, even at the best of times, has never been easy. "I was angry," Marj says in that matter-of-fact way that you feel she might use to report a global apocalypse. "But I knew that I could get it done because she had before me. I owed that to my daughter, her dad, myself and my family before me. Then I just put my head down and went to work."

⌒

ALMOST noon now, and Marj is in her Yukon, one of seven trucks I count. They, along with the various tractors, skidders and trailers, make up the vehicular fleet of Veno Ranches and McArthur Livestock. The vehicles are stored in a big metal Quonset hut in the farmyard. I discover there's a whole world out there. Off to the right, big metal granaries hold pellets of cattle feed. To the rear, half-ton bales of hay that don't last as long as you'd think in a place where each cow eats thirty pounds per day for feed. Farther yonder, a corral made out of discarded Alberta Energy poles, a cattle scale for weighing livestock and chutes for loading the cows into trucks and trailers.

The latter is next to the red barn that was here when she and Greg bought the place. Built in 1918, the structure was the handiwork of the ranch's original homesteader, Gottlieb Knopp. When the old fella and his wife died, the ranch went to a daughter, who married badly—a drinker and poker player who let the place run down. They eventually sold it to a rancher named Jack Jager, who let things slide even more, until he sold it to Marj and Greg in 1980. "The place was a run-down mess," says Marj, "but with lots of enthusiasm and hard work we cleaned it up and built new buildings and corrals and fences when we could afford them." Marj, Greg and her dad straightened the barn themselves. Now the barn loft's floor is plumb enough for their annual square dance and cattle auction. When they were done with the barn renovation, a neighbour said that old Knopp would sure be proud of it, as he was a proud, hard-working man.

In short-grass country endurance and fortitude are treated with a reverence akin to an ability to profitably flip a condo among city folks. Calling someone hard-working—along with saying they are honest and have integrity, which matters in a place where deals are still done on a handshake—is the highest praise you can have for a person. Being a survivor is something to feel good about too. The number of cattle farms in Alberta shrank from eighty thousand in 1941 to under twenty-nine thousand in 2006. Farms are getting bigger. But farmers are getting older—Alberta had 16,660 farmers under the age of thirty-five in 1991 versus 6,290 by 2006. It's harder to get out of the business when land prices are so high and there's less and less appetite among the young for the kind of labour that cattle ranching requires.

Marj has always liked a daylight start: because she's fondest of the world at that hour but also because cattle ranching is what economists like to call "labour intensive" toil. Toil is my word, not Marj's. That's simply not how she sees things. Spring, when the two-year-old heifers calve, may mean a parade of eighteen-hour days wrestling with half-ton animals out in the calving pasture. It may mean checking every head of cattle daily and new calves twice or even three times in the run of twenty-four hours. ("No daylight," she tells me, "is wasted.") But she thinks of it as "a time of rejuvenation. The air smells so fresh, the crocuses are growing, everything is new and fresh and young."

Don't expect her to complain, either, about the summer days, which also start before light, since it's the easiest time to check the cattle and the mosquitoes aren't buzzing yet. To hear her tell it, no better time can be had on this earth than when dozens of family members descend on the ranch for the annual ritual of branding the calves in June. Things get easier in the fall, when they get the hay in, fix the corrals, vaccinate the calves and wean them from their mothers. The rest of the time is spent preparing for winter, during which she says the cows "pretty much take care of themselves"—a statement that I discover is not quite true.

It is, by Alberta standards, a balmy minus two farrenheit by the time we set out. Normally Marj would have her rifle propped up in the passenger seat. Since I'm there, we're unarmed as we take a right past the grey mailbox that just says "R.R. 1 Hanna, Alberta." We pass her two saddle horses— Yikes, who is reddish, Vegas, mostly black, and a donkey that goes by Jenny inside a fence close to the road. Marj hangs a left and stops. In a greenish canvas jacket, yellow work gloves and pull-on rain boots, she gets out to open the gate.

This is the "West Place" ranch, since expanded from the original Jager land, where she, daughter Janet and son-in-law Steven run three hundred pairs of cows and calves year-round. To keep predators out and the cattle in, their three ranches have sixty-nine miles of three- or five-strand barbed wire fencing, strung between wooden posts sunk sixteen feet apart. At sixty-nine cents a foot, that's one of their biggest costs. So part of every day is spent splicing damaged fence or, when it's beyond repair, rebuilding the entire section.

A dozen or so scattered heifers and calves give us the eye. And well they should: in time the good-quality ones, along with young yearling bulls, will be sold to other ranchers for breeding. Steers (castrated bulls) and older heifers go to feed-lots to be fattened for slaughter. It's a Darwinian world on a cattle ranch; producers need to get rid of animals that lower the genetic quality of the herd. So Marj is always examining the cow-calf pairs to see which ones are doing well and which ones aren't. "That time pays off when it is culling time," she explains. Each year around 10 percent of her breeding herd is sold at an auction.

As we walk around, Marj tells me that she's looking for other things too. "You've got to know, are they satisfied?" she says. "Are they wandering too much? If they're wandering too much, they're looking for something. They need minerals. They need salt. They need grass. Maybe the water is dirty." She fiddles with a siphon, capable of moving eleven to twelve gallons of water from a coulee to a water trough every thirty seconds when wide open. Then she scrambles down an incline, shovel in hand. She keeps talking as she chops a water hole in the ice for the cattle. Marj has got a bad back and on days like today feels the chill in her bones, several of which have been broken in on-the-job mishaps. But ranches die without water.

They also need grass. It takes two years for a calf to reach full size, which is 1,200 to 1,400 pounds for a cow and a little less for a bull. Cows, as we know, have a fairly narrow range of activities. They sleep, they stare, they move their bowels, they wander slowly around. Occasionally, when scared, they take off with a little gallop. Mostly, in their own distinctive way, they eat. They swallow grass. The food comes back up into their mouths as cud, which they chew again. Because Marj's cattle spend most of the year out on the pasture, it takes thirty acres of grassland to raise a single head of cattle.

Back on dry land she uses her hand to ruffle snow off the ground cover. At the "Home Place," a trio of creeks meet on a large flood plain that is naturally irrigated during spring runoff or during large rainfalls. The 2000–2009 period brought droughts, complete with associated grasshopper infestations, rivalling those seen by her grandparents. The past three years, though, were characterized by better-than-average rain and decent winter snowfalls. Consequently, her cattle have had lots of prairie wool, a hardy and nutritious native grass for grazing.

Some things have changed a lot since her grandparents first broke ground in this area, Marj says. Being able to "read the grass" is 100 percent the same. "You have to understand what time of year cattle prefer what kind of grass. Tame grass, the stuff reseeded by man, is typically at its best in the late spring and early summer," she says. "You'd better be using that then if you've got some and then save your prairie grass for this time of year, because that's when it shines. It's great stuff to winter cows on. They stay healthy. There's lots of minerals and lots of nutrients in it. It's just something you learn."

～

WE'RE back in the truck, heading east, then north, then east again. From the looks of it we could turn southward and, except for the occasional cross fence, not hit a single thing until we reached Cessford, where the Nesters still farm. Shifting down and up, Marj tells me how her dad, Jack, stayed in school until grade eight, then began driving teams of horses and pitching bundles of hay like his brothers. His first trip to Calgary was to enlist in the Canadian army after receiving his conscription letter. He served in Britain and northwest Europe from February 1943 until he was discharged three years later. Then he came back to work the family farm.

On the way home he passed ghost towns, abandoned homesteads and shells of grain elevators. So many people just up and left from southeastern Alberta during the Dirty Thirites that the provincial government moved in to administer vast regions of the dry belt that no longer could sustain themselves. In 1938 three "special areas" were created to be administered by the provincially run Special Areas Board. Newcomers with the stomach for it could purchase twenty-year leases for abandoned lands. In the early 1950s, Jack acquired 2,560 acres on the Berry Creek, which was in Special Area 2.

"It was just a dot," says Marj. "There was a grain elevator. A little country school where fourteen was the biggest class ever. I still remember being amazed at all the other school buses and kids on my first day of grade one. But you are who you are and it was a great place to grow up." When opportunity knocked, Jack added to the farm. Marj remembers her mom Lillian's big garden on the ranch homestead, the parade of family dogs and the saddle horses—Sandy, Dixie and Starr—which were the main mode of transportation for her and her brother.

There were only two other girls in the area. So Marj grew up rough and tough, doing what the boys did. "Chasing cattle, feeding cows, butchering beef, chickens and pigs, helping get the milk cow in so that Jack could milk her." They fished in the creek beside their house. The kids taught her how to play fastball and hockey and to go tobogganing. "I would go and check cattle with Dad on horseback, always watching the wildlife, learning to respect the weather," she says.

She finished high school and got a job for a while in an accounting office. ("I learned what I didn't want to be," she says. "I was inside all of the time. I felt like a gopher.") At nineteen she married Greg Veno, who grew up about forty miles northwest of the Nester place, but went to high school in Cessford. He and Marj met on the school bus. "We had similar backgrounds," she recalls. "We both knew how to laugh and have a lot of fun while we worked or whatever we were doing. We were best friends before we were anything and remained best friends through thick and thin."

For five years they managed a feedlot near Bassano. It was enlightening to be around the owner, Bud Stewart, who showed them how to feed cattle to butcher weight, how to deal with meat packers and how to hedge cattle stocks on the commodities market to protect against prices heading the wrong way. Marj calls what they learned a "university-class education that no school could offer at the time." But they were kids with dreams. They wanted to keep the family narrative moving forward. And then they heard about this land.

⌒

WHEN Greg died, Marj knew she couldn't keep raising cattle and growing wheat by herself. So she bought some grass and hayseed. That first spring her dad, nephew and brother-in-law helped her seed all the farmland to hay and grass for the cattle. The rain helped: twenty-one inches the first year and eighteen each for the next two years. Getting rid of the crops allowed her to trade in her combine for a new haybine, a baler and a baler-mower. She bought Angus bulls to crossbreed with the two hundred Limousin cows she already owned. Then she used the resulting crossbred heifer calves to build her herd up to three hundred cows. Marj called the result "cattle that work for me, not me for them." For the next five years she and her daughter, Janet, worked the range, cutting and baling the hay and raising the cattle. "The days were long—daylight to dark," says Marj. "But hard work kept me sane. Or at least, I thought I was."

Her focus, besides keeping the farm afloat, was ensuring that Janet got to play sports and do the other things teenage kids got to do. That meant a major dose of empty nest syndrome when her daughter—often the only person Marj saw during the workweek—headed off to college in Lethbridge. Worried about becoming "some kind of kooky eccentric," Marj found a young guy who wanted to learn, please excuse me, the ropes of cattle ranching. She put him on the payroll and gave his family and him a place to live. That took the pressure off Janet to come home on weekends to help out. It also gave Marj the leeway to have a life. At a bull sale in 1995 she met Murray, a cattleman from Ontario who had taken to raising Angus beef in the Chauvin area of Alberta. "As time passed he became a permanent fixture" is how Marj sums up the courtship. They married in 1998.

Our feet make a bubble-wrap noise as we traverse East Place, where the ground is sandy and covered with lots of natural bush. The water table is uncommonly high for this country: the dugouts are spring fed; the water wells are about a hundred feet deep but never run dry. That allows Marj and Murray to raise 180 cow-calf pairs and a hundred yearling heifers for nine months of the year here. Marj knows what she can get for her cattle: $3,500 or $3,600 for a breeding bull, sixty to seventy cents per pound for a slaughter cow and $1,200 to $1,500 for a heifer. She also knows that profit margins are variable depending upon a whole range of factors: the world market for beef, how much supply is out there, the public perception of her product. In other words, they are price takers rather than makers, in economics-speak. So the easiest way to maximize profits is by keeping costs down and timing the market so that she sells on the price highs, not the lows.

Marj checks the gate—the start of deer season is days off—and considers the water holes. Then she looks northward, stands straight and says, "I think that's a bull moose." Marj gets out her binoculars, scopes the animal a couple of hundred yards away. She says, "Oh yeah, that's a bull moose," then hands the glasses to me. There turn out to be two of them. We trade the glasses back and forth, watching them grapple using their antlers for dominance. Marj tries to get their attention with a moose call. We can't tell, from this distance, if they notice or not. But after a while they saunter off.

This isn't the sort of thing I see every day. For Marj, who likes the wild better than cities, it is. "You get to see nature from the perspective of how it really is," she says of her life. "It isn't in a zoo or a book. It's out there. It's pretty easy to drive by at sixty miles an hour and not even see that stuff. Just slow down and take your time and you see that little three-point buck that was standing at the gate."

At which point I ask myself—what little three-point buck? For that reason, I vow to try paying attention when we get back in the truck. Whether it's the focus or just coincidence, all of a sudden animal life is everywhere: an owl sitting on a big rock, a weird little bird that Marj tells me is a prairie chicken, a coyote that lives another day because Marj doesn't have her rifle with her today. The three ranches, she tells me, support mule deer, antelope and, during the last ten years or so, more moose and elk. Marj says the Hungarian partridge, which I gather is some kind of pheasant, finds good habitat to thrive there regardless of coyotes and foxes. Her land is also on the main migratory flight path of the Canada goose and millions of ducks, which like to drop in.

In a copse of trees near the road she slows down to point out a pair of white-tailed deer. They freeze for a minute, then bound away as others join them. By the time the last one disappears I've counted twenty-seven. I realize that could be more than the total of all the deer I've glimpsed in the wild in my lifetime.

WEST Place, which Marj owns herself, is twenty miles off. The occasional gas well—ugly, black and often fenced off— breaks the ice-frosted grassy plain. Ranchers only own the surface rights of the land; what's underneath is the possession of the province of Alberta, which auctions off the mineral rights. Gas wells are a real pain in the ass if something goes wrong, Marj says. Most of the time, the ranchers are happy for the royalty the well operator pays them.

Once your eyes get accustomed you can tell that it wasn't always so empty around here. Some of the old homesteads— the ones abandoned when their owners gave up hope, were starved out or went broke back in the early thirties—are just a remnant of a wall, a foundation or a corral now. In others, abandoned more recently, it's like a set for *The Walking Dead*: skeletons of old trucks in the yard, pigeons flying in and out through broken windows. Some people just couldn't take the isolation, the economic uncertainty. They blew their brains out with dope or booze or their guns. Or, in most cases, one day they just left.

When she and Greg moved into the area thirty-two years ago, it wasn't exactly Yonge and Bloor in Toronto. They had neighbours. But a lot of them were getting up there, wanted to retire and had no kids interested in the farming or ranching life. Or they had financial issues that forced them to sell out and try something else. All told, forty families who used to live on or around her land have packed up and vamoosed since she arrived. "Leonard and Martha Faupel sold to us and another neighbour to retire in 1989," she says, running through the list. "Clarence Heggen wanted to retire 1988. Ed Housch retired sometime in the late eighties. Hector Lloyd moved on to other things in 2002 or 2003. Eric Walper moved on to other things 2000. Wayne Faupel moved to another area to farm in 1996."

It's about 3 p.m. The sky is darkening and the temperature dropping as we make a little detour. There's nothing remotely derelict about the Senkiw Ukrainian Orthodox Church. It's white, small and wooden, with a gabled roof topped by a small cupola bearing a mounted cross. The windows are glassed in, the small cemetery next to it neat and orderly. Senkiw is the surname of lots of settlers from the western Ukraine who settled in Alberta and Manitoba. Someone somewhere still looks after the church, which I'm guessing still holds services when a Ukrainian cleric makes his way to these parts. Also well maintained is the graveyard next door, where I imagine a lot of those Senkiws are buried, which adds a mournful quality of the scene.

When Marj and Greg bought West Place from old Leonard Faupel in 1989, it was about a third of the size it is now. It was also mostly a wheat farm. "I knew what I knew best," she says, "and it wasn't farming." Now the prairie grass from the seed they planted feeds two hundred cow-calf pairs year-round. The ranch is gently rolling prairie with some bluffs of poplar and willow trees. Marj shows me coulees and one heck of a dam, which we look at for a minute before hustling back to the truck.

We zig and zag. Eventually we hit a long stretch of straight road on which something moving approaches from the other direction. It turns out to be a friend of Marj's named Sue who is clad in a snowsuit. Her husband, John, is away hauling in hay for the winter, so Sue is heading to a friend's place for dinner. She's on foot even though the friend, whose place we passed, lives some five miles away by my reckoning. We chat for a moment. Then she picks up where she left off, long strides chewing up the road, a singular figure heading cheerfully into the open prairie.

Back at the Home Place, Marj shows me the inside of the barn, which is patrolled by eight comical border collie puppies that slip and slide on the upstairs loft floor like it's a sheet of ice. When she and Murray hold their spring bull sale, the proceedings take place here, where the guests look at videos of the bulls penned outside. At other times, an old-style country and western band sets up in the loft. Friends, neighbours and family two-step into the night.

Tradition, like history, matters to Marj. From the walls of the loft, it's obvious that she's proud of her people, how they've carried on and what they've done. In a place of honour hangs a 2009 poster celebrating "100 years of ranching in the Special Areas by the family of Hugh and Evelyn Nester." There are old black-and-white pictures of the Home Place as it was in 1954, long before Marj owned it; of her dad hauling loose hay in 1949 with a four-horse hitch. Over there is Hugh Nester's homestead, *circa* 1912, before he married Evelyn. (A cousin of Marj's still owns and operates the original property.)

I come upon a more recent, colour photo of Marj's people: her mom and dad with Marj and Murray, along with daughter Janet and son-in-law Steven. The couple have a farm in Gleichen, Alberta, where they maintain a feedlot for fattening calves for market, run 250 cow-calf pairs and grow barley, canola and hay. Steven's dad is dead. His mom lives nearby on her own land. Janet and Steven also own some grassland that attaches to Marj's West Place. The couple consequently farm and ranch in conjunction with their family on both sides.

Also in the photo are Janet and Steven's two boys, the apples of their grandmother's eye. Tate is eight. He sounds like a chip off the old block: roping and riding in kid rodeos, riding along with Marj as she works, asking the same type of questions she used to ask her daddy. Wyatt, two years younger, is quieter and takes a bit of a back seat to his older brother. He's more interested in a ranch's machinery and building things than the livestock. But Marj can see the pair of them with her and Murray's land when they are done. "Family traditions run deep," she says, "and there is a lot of pride in keeping those alive."

Youngsters like that are getting rarer and rarer in this day when most Canadian kids think that milk comes from a carton in a store. Canuck boys and girls don't put chin in hands, peer at the cereal bowl and reflect that the Cap'n Crunch wouldn't be there if not for some Saskatchewan grain farmer working his ass off in the blazing sun. Just as their parents probably don't remember that some time ago among their people existed someone growing something on a country farm.

Marj understands that people don't necessarily want to live close to the land anymore; she really does. "Young couples today—and I see it with my daughter and her family, who want to go to the show, want to take the kids to hockey games every week—they don't want to put the time in," she says. "They work hard. But I don't think most people have the dedication and the drive to stick to it to get through the rough spots and ride it out."

She's at the table in the ranch house kitchen. The kettle is on. Marj, by her own admission, is cash poor but asset rich: they don't have hundreds of thousands in the bank. But they do have a lot of land that has soared in value in the thirty-two years they've owned it. In 1982 they paid fifty-five dollars an acre for the leased grassland and two hundred dollars an acre for the cultivated farmland. Now the leased grassland would easily go for three hundred dollars an acre and the cultivated farmland four-fifty to five hundred dollars an acre. There are areas, in fact, where those prices would qualify as a bargain.

Which goes a long way to explaining why young people no longer dream of getting themselves a ranch. "It isn't fiscally responsible for a young couple to borrow the kind of money they would have to borrow to buy an outfit that they could make a living off of and raise their family on. They will never on God's green earth pay the debt off."

She goes on, "You really have to want to do it. There's ups and downs, but you'd better figure twenty years. That's the reality. The best work years of your life—that's what it is going to take to come out the other end and be sitting where I'm sitting."

Marj, on the other hand, never really wanted anything else. She had a dream. It's not a dream that speaks to new starts. Or, even in the early years of the twenty-first century, a dazzling future. Her dream was simple: to have a family. To honour her lineage as an Alberta cattle rancher—and follow the forward-ho example set by her parents and grandparents. To rise every day and ride out into this hard, beautiful land. To endure.

CHAPTER
EIGHT

LIFE OF A SALESMAN

YEARS ago, long before his hair turned a lavish silver and he peered pensively over reading glasses perched on the bridge of his pug nose, Steve Forbes took a Saturday job at Noel Kerr's men's and ladies' clothing store in downtown Ottawa. "I was just fifteen, which is a little young to be working the floor selling shirts, ties and the like," he says. "I guess I did like talking." It was 1969. Man walked on the moon; countries waged war in Southeast Asia; terrorists bombed stock exchanges. Kids everywhere were riled up—marching on governments, rioting in the halls of universities. Yet you wouldn't know that the world was aflame standing inside Noel Kerr's place.

Picture Steve—white dress shirt, dark slacks, flashy tie and spit-polish penny loafers—as the radiators hummed to dull

Ottawa's bone-snapping cold. Imagine him that first day on the job, standing there as the bank manager, the Parliament Hill functionary or the high school principal walked down the rows of merchandise. At that point Steve had never been kissed, and when he borrowed his dad's stainless steel razor, it was really only wishful thinking. The man he approached could have survived Juno Beach or the great polio epidemic of '53. If Steve had thought about it for long enough, he might just have lost his nerve. He might have headed into the backroom and shuffled some boxes around until the customers left. He might have just said, "Aw, the heck with it," told Mr. Kerr that he wasn't cut out for this, and then just walked out the door.

Except Steve's father had met his mom when they worked as models for the venerable Eaton's catalogue. In the midst of North America's postwar economic boom, Art Forbes got a job selling Heinz ketchup—"picked, cooked and bottled the same day"—throughout Ontario. A few years later, with five mouths to feed, he took a position with the Biltmore Hat Company, which made the official headgear of the Royal Canadian Mounted Police as well as the hat of choice for the nation's businessmen. Later he joined the John Forsyth Shirt Company, with its motto that "no one ever regretted buying quality." There he did well enough that head office moved the whole clan to Ottawa so Art could build the brand throughout the Ottawa Valley.

Steve Forbes isn't sure if this backstory made it inevitable that his calling would be as a salesman. He just knows that on that 1969 morning, instead of quitting, he walked across the store and, in a voice just starting to break, said, "Good morning, sir. What can I help you with today?" And that forty-two years later he still is, in his low-key way, always closing.

At fifty-six, Steve now has a round face and chesty build to go with his forthright manner. He lives in a straightforward world where people pay their bills, help their neighbours and are loyal to their friends. He calls his wife, Anne, "honey," and still refers to his late dad as "Father." Yet the gold bling around Steve's neck, and his thick wristwatch, let you know that he's been to the city. That he's a man who understands the importance of appearances. A man who, for long stretches, made a living by convincing store owners that the shirts, sports jackets and accessories he sold were the best damn shirts, sports jackets and accessories available, because otherwise, well, Steve Forbes wouldn't touch them with a ten-foot pole, would he.

Once he lived on the road, eating at Formica-topped diner tables, guzzling rank coffee from travel cups, sleeping in motel rooms that stank of cigarettes. Now his workweek consists of a series of day trips that end at home with the people he loves. It's Monday, which means he will be heading west, along Route 148 in western Quebec, bound for the municipality of Bryson before moving on to Campbell's Bay, Fort Coulonge, Ladysmith, Quyon and Bristol—a counter-clockwise loop of about 160 kilometres. Tuesday he heads east toward cottage country. Shawville, which is in Quebec but not really of it, gets all of Wednesday. Steve spends Thursday making his deliveries. Friday is cleanup day: he handles any leftover deliveries, gets quotes on special orders and goes out to see any customers who need a little hand-holding.

The township of Pontiac—in some parts so beautiful it makes a person's breath go short, in other parts just good farmland—is the biggest township in Quebec. But the last time I looked it had only one traffic light, at an intersection where a pair of banks, the town hall and a sandstone building of undetermined use meet, in "downtown" Shawville. The town was founded in 1873 by Tipperary Protestants, mercifully dissuaded from naming the town Daggville after one of the pioneer families. All those years later, this isn't one of those places the federal government points to when it talks about Canada being a multicultural melting pot. The business owners are still named O'Neill, Hodgins, Tracey and Kelly. There's a Killarney's Bar and a Mickey McGuire Equipment. The 2006 census shows that 1,070 of Shawville's 1,490 residents spoke only English and that only ten of the town's residents called themselves visible minorities. Fully 75 percent of the folks who live here describe themselves as Protestants—high in Roman Catholic Quebec. It's thus perhaps not too surprising that Shawville has had its run-ins with the province's Office québécois de la langue française for transgressing the province's language laws—most notably in 1999, when a posse of militant Shawville English speakers chased a provincial "language police" inspector out of town during a faceoff over French on business signs.

At the corner of Centre and King stands a wooden, white three-storey building with a peaked roof and black shutters. The Shawville Academy Building has been there since the 1850s. The *Equity*, the "voice of Pontiac" and the area's sole weekly newspaper, arrived some sixty years later. Steve starts most workdays in the print shop on the ground floor of the building. Newspapering has become one of those troubled industries where only the quick survive. When the *Equity*'s presses aren't busy turning out broadsheet papers, they print invoice statements, bill books, wedding invitations, luncheon napkins, health and gun registry cards, address labels, passports and personalized forms. Steve sells those. He will sell you an order of pizza menus, personalized stationery or some school pictures. He also sells classified ads—"ten dollars for fifteen words in advance, fifteen cents for each additional word"—and display ads in the *Equity* and its annual travel guide.

"The truth is," he says, "whatever you really want I can get." The evidence is piled around his desk: garbage bags, toilet paper, paper towels, dishwasher and laundry detergent. Steve, who is paid a salary, will sell you a big bottle of heavy-duty industrial or kitchen cleaner, a tub of disinfectant or a bag of road salt. He will sell you some floor stripper, a bottle of gel to clean a deep fryer and liquids for cleaning a toilet bowl or scrubbing a tub. He peddles printer and photocopier toner and cartridges. He leases dishwashers. He sells books by local authors with titles like *Campfire Ghost Stories*, *Bugs of Ontario*, *Poems of the Pontiac* and *Counting Frogs and Eating Crow*. If you need a sign—"Ask if it's Canadian Beef," "Movies, CDs, PlayStation & Antiques"—he's your man. Need pens and notepads? Just ask Steve. Want a fax machine or a laser printer? In Pontiac there's really only one place to look. Relocating and need something to stuff the moving boxes with? Steve's your boy for that too.

He arrives at the *Equity* building at around seven every weekday morning, puts on the coffee, checks his emails, then shoots the breeze with Heather Dickson, the statuesque owner, and whoever else has rolled in. At around nine he walks into the parking lot and climbs into his Ford minivan. He makes a couple of dickey turns through town and pulls in behind a hardware store that has been there for more than a century and a half. Steve's father-in-law, Mick Hodgins, owns the business. All bone and gristle, he still stacks shelves at eighty-one. Mick's son Ronnie works there, as do his three daughters, including Steve's wife, Anne.

Steve confers with her for a moment. Then he's back in the van, turning the ignition. It may be a beautiful summer morning, mid-twenties, in La Belle Province. But it is also 9:22 a.m. and money doesn't grow on trees for people in his profession. "In the whole world of trade and commerce probably no one has so hard and baffling a job as a traveling salesman," W. Francis Gates wrote in *Tips for the Traveling Salesman,* which was published in the Great Depression, before fax machines, the Internet, big-box stores and the other things that now threaten the salesman's life. Knowing the product line was never enough, Gates felt. A salesman has to know human nature. He has to persuade with logic and sway with hustle and desire. He has to believe in possibility, that he will do just fine. Because when you start each day on the loose, with just open road ahead, you have to believe in something. Steve most of all believes in Steve.

⌒

THERE was a time, after the rise of mass manufacturing on this continent, when men like Steve arrived on foot. When they came like David Epstein, who showed up in the coal towns of Cape Breton in 1907, penniless and unable to speak a word of English, and began to "peddle" for his uncle Morris. "I had a seventy-five-pound pack on my back and a fifty-pound pack in front," he recalled years later. "I walked house to house from [Cape] Smokey to Bay St. Lawrence." That's some sixty kilometres through the raw highlands of Cape Breton. The turn-of-the-century peddlers who trudged into Newfoundland's outports walked even farther. Their bags packed with things unavailable in the local merchant stores—stationery, pencils, combs, ties, handkerchiefs, tobacco, tea, shirts and pocket knives—they sometimes covered more than thirty kilometres a day on foot in search of sales.

In western Canada "Syrian" peddlers were "something of an institution," wrote Gilbert Johnson. "Sometimes on foot, with a pack on his back and a case of trinkets and small wares in his hand, but more often with a horse and a light wagon in summer, or with a sleigh in winter, he traveled the prairie trails on more or less regular routes."

In early-twentieth-century Ontario, bells heralded the peddler's arrival. Then, as Andrew Armitage wrote in the [Owen Sound, Ontario] *Sun Times*, "up the lane he came, his wagon bristling with rakes, hoes, tin dishes, brooms, needles and thread, iron kettles and milk pans. Spring was the best time to be and out about, peddling. The long winter just passed would have exhausted many a farm wife's supplies and worn out at least one of her cooking utensils."

These travelling men came from a long lineage. In England they were known as "hawkers," "canvassers," "cheapjacks," "mongers," "laniers" or "pushers." Some were called "rag-and-bone men"—my personal favourite—because they collected old rags for converting into fabric and paper, as well as bones for making glue and other stuff they could trade. Householders knew they were coming because they rang a bell, or called out, in a singsong fashion, something that sounded like "rag and bone."

It was thus only natural that peddlers would become common sights throughout pioneer Canada. Benita Baker wrote in the *Beaver* that in the early days, many of them, particularly the Jewish rag-and-bone men, were shunned as scavengers and beggars and equated with bogeymen who stole children. Signs were posted stating "No Beggars or Peddlers Allowed." Former Ontario cabinet minister Allan Grossman's father was a rag-and-bone man. In his autobiography, Grossman recalled that "it was almost a daily occurrence for father to have stones thrown at him or have his beard pulled by young hoodlums, sometimes encouraged by adults."

In 1912, *Maclean's* magazine described the junk dealer's pitiful lot:

> ... the sheeny you can see frequenting the lanes and uttering raucous cries of "rags, bones and bottles. Any rags today lady?" They are usually dressed in clothing that was made for somebody else and are adorned . . . with whiskers . . . Little hunch-backed cigarette-smoking men, they are out with their push carts shortly after daylight, and they continue their toil many hours after the union Canadian workman has gone home for the night. The calves of their legs are familiar with dogs' fangs; other parts of their bodies are acquainted with Christian boots, yet . . . how joyfully they toil . . . Most of them have come to us from Russia where their lives were never safe.

In other words, they endured. The early peddler was more than a "department store on wheels" or a "mobile five and dime store," supplying the needs of everyday life to isolated rural folk. He was also a tinsmith with talents who could fix old teakettles and pans and turn them into something useful. He could do skilled carpentry work. He sold bibles, almanacs full of tips for the farm, school readers, even handbooks on animal doctoring, home hygiene and manners. From the back of his wagon he flogged apple stock, cuttings of mulberry and gooseberry and new strains of fruits and perennials. Going door to door, he sold stoves, ranges and patent medicine. He even acted as a kind of travelling bard, Armitage wrote: "The peddler broke the solitude of a lonely farm existence with happy gossip of neighbor just far enough away that the farm-bound wife may not have met them except through the peddler's patter."

When the train came to Canada, travellers filled the rail cars. At each whistle stop Steve's predecessors jumped off to see their customers and then on again when the conductor blew his whistle, signalling impending departure. Come nightfall they took their leisure in hotel restaurants and bars; men in crisp suits, cigarette smoke laying a haze across the room, as they exchanged gossip about who the good customers were and where the new prospects were to be found.

The Great Depression brought more men into the ranks of commercial travellers. Then came the boom following the Second World War. By 1950, Canada's three commercial travellers associations had roughly one hundred thousand members. Unofficial estimates reach four times as high. That's a head-spinning number considering that the country's population was about fifteen million at that time. "They sold everything," says Terry Carruthers, chief executive officer of the North West Commercial Travellers' Association of Canada, which today represents all the travelling salesmen in Atlantic Canada and west of Ontario. "You look at any kind of operation—no matter how big or small—and at one point they had a traveller on the road acting as their sales rep."

It is hard to see the life as glamorous. Carruthers's outfit was formed in 1882 because so many travelling salesmen were dying in hotel fires that their destitute families needed an insurance policy to cover the cost of getting their bodies home. During the heyday of the travelling salesman most of them spent fifty weeks a year on the road. The average salesman lived in one province and covered the two provinces on either side. Some had even bigger territories—the Maritimes through to Toronto, Vancouver to Thunder Bay. A lot of the travellers would work in tandem. One selling, say, soap for Procter and Gamble would show up in a prairie town and take orders for his own products as well as for a dry goods guy in the employ of Canada Packers—who, at that very moment might have been three hundred miles away returning the favour. When they met up again later on, they would simply swap orders. Everybody would be happy.

In time the travelling salesmen morphed into "account executives" and "district managers." Whatever their titles they were still salesmen. They were still a brotherhood—and, eventually, a sisterhood as more and more women joined their ranks—even if Arthur Miller's play had turned them into a depressing symbol of the hypocrisy and faded dreams of the industrial age. That clearly wasn't how they saw themselves as they pointed their fin-backed sedans toward the horizon. By hitting the open road with an empty order book, they had no choice but to live in the moment. They were out there, unfettered, without a safety net, the embodiment of Adam

Smith's freewheeling capitalist dream. Until along came the fax machine and screwed everything up.

⌒

A BIG paper mill used to be the main employer in these parts. Now the road to Bryson is mostly just empty blacktop lined by spruce and pine until we reach the municipal buildings. Any salesman will tell you that making the right entrance is critical to success. Too pushy and you turn customers off; too meek and you don't get past the front desk. I discover that Steve, who by conservative estimate has made something near sixty thousand pitches to customers, and conceivably many more than that, has a mastery of what Gates considers the first rule of salesmanship: make every call personal. He enters the room like Norm in *Cheers*—a familiar figure talking fast in a flat alto. "What's up? What's new? There he is," he says. "They haven't fired you yet. Amazing! I mean it." He customarily greets people by nickname—"Hammerhead," "Annie Oakley," "Doc" (who is actually a dentist), "Webster" (because he seems to have an answer for everyone—just like the dictionary) and "Steve" (whose name actually seems to be Billy). The Purolator delivery guy is known as "Puro." One female customer is called "Happy," which, from the looks of it, may just be Steve being funny.

Generally speaking, only reporters, lawyers, auto mechanics and telemarketers can rival travelling salesmen when it comes to being held in low public esteem. I find it noteworthy then that when Steve makes his presence known, nobody visibly cringes or whispers *sotto voce*, "Christ, him again." People look up, wave, nod and then go back to work.

The municipality's director-general, Tracy Herault, makes her way up to the front desk. She and Steve banter a little about things a stranger simply cannot follow. When actual business is transacted, it happens so quickly that you almost miss it.

"Paper towels?"

"Two packages."

"Garbage bags? Toilet paper?"

"No, I guess we're okay."

Back in the car Steve takes out a mini-cassette recorder, punches some buttons and repeats the order—"Two packages of paper towels for Bryson"—into the mike. The procedure still seems new to him. When he started out, orders were scribbled down in a rough notebook, then, back at the office, transcribed onto a proper order form, which was mailed or couriered to the manufacturer. Now, at the end of the day he hits the replay button, writes the orders out in pen and then faxes them in to the supplier.

There's an irony there. When the fax machine arrived in the 1980s, a lot of companies concluded that customers would simply fax their orders in. Many salesmen—both freelancers and reps on staff at particular commercial concerns—lost their jobs. When the Internet came along, a lot more of them had to find a new line of work. Getting rid of those salaries immediately improved the bottom line of companies. But when sales started dropping, the owners couldn't quite figure out why. "They finally realized there was value in a sales-person who walks in and sits down across the table and says, 'This is what I'm selling,'" notes Carruthers. "Feel its weight. This is what you will get from me. I will be back every four to six weeks. If there is a problem, I will be back."

Some of the smart marketers agreed and rehired some sales agents. Independents like Steve who handle a number of different product lines are still a dying breed. The small independent retail stores are going out of business; big-box store chains buy their products in huge volumes at trade shows in Vegas rather than from salesmen walking through the door. Real relationships between sellers and buyers—cemented over hundreds of visits over perhaps a couple of generations—are now as passé as Rotary Club lunches. The North West Commercial Travellers' Association—the country's largest commercial travellers' organization—now has just five thousand members. Most of them are paid entirely by commission.

Steve, with a salary, is one of the lucky ones. He mostly looks after existing customers, rather than prospecting for new ones. With the closest Wal-Mart twenty minutes away, a need still exists in his corner of the Pontiac for someone willing to come to the client. For how long that need will exist is undetermined. A little luck and Steve might make it to retirement.

For now it's a pretty good life. Steve and Anne live in a 1,500-square-foot bungalow by the banks of the Ottawa River. Every year they get two weeks in Florida and every decade they buy a new car. When the weather improves, they cruise around in their 115 Yamaha on the Ottawa River or sit out under the stars in their backyard hot tub. They're close to the people who matter to them. On the weekend their house crawls with friends. The step-kids from Anne's first marriage—and the five grandchildren—live nearby. On the first Monday of every month Steve makes his way to Bristol Town Hall; there, as one of the municipality's seven councillors, he considers such matters as where to put deer crossing signs and how to prevent thumb tacks from damaging the walls at town hall.

Steve flips on the radio: MAJIC 100, an Ottawa soft-rock station. He keeps to the speed limit, which is good, since he's soon pulling into the parking lot at the Sûreté du Québec in Campbell's Bay. As he shoots the breeze with the youngish commander and his detective wife, not a word is said about business. By his very presence, though, Steve is checking up on his customer, building goodwill and fostering loyalty. Because that is how a man gets to grow old in this business.

Moments later, a little farther down the road, Steve is inside one of the Campbell's Bay's municipal buildings, jawing with a woman named Natasha. Years ago some big American company tried writing out spiels, which their travelling salesman had to memorize and recite to customers. Steve wouldn't have lasted a day mouthing someone else's lines. Hearing him talk to a customer is like eavesdropping on a meandering conversation that began, say, fifteen years ago. They gossip and kid. Steve brings up stuff that wound-tight city folk would find unnecessary, perhaps even irritating. As an afterthought—in much the way Peter Falk as Colombo would stop in the doorway and say, "Just one more thing"— he looks back over his shoulder while heading for the exit and asks, "Need anything?"

What I mean to say is that Steve is no practitioner of the hard sell. He's no Sam Slick, the Connecticut clock dealer, putting a timepiece in every farmhouse he visited, through flattery and bullshit; or Willy Loman, embodying all the false promise of the American Dream in a push for another sale. Steve can make a compelling case for his products because, even after all those years on the road, his enthusiasm for the things is undimmed. He stands there and his aw-shucks smile, easy body language and self-deprecating manner seem to say, "No pressure whatsoever. I'm just here to help if I can." But look closely: the scent of the sale makes his eyes shine and his shoulders bulge. His fingers, I swear, grow a couple of ring sizes.

Natasha, it turns out, wants file folders, staples, pens, some signs, garbage bags and paper towels. That's precisely the order he takes at his next stop, the Pontiac's business development agency, before we drive through some flat Quebec farmland and pull into Gigi's Café for some coffee. Two Sûreté du Québec police officers and a table of housewives sit in the roomy interior. An approned lady—Gigi?—greets him from behind the counter. Steve orders a doughnut and a cup of coffee, which he douses liberally with cream and sugar (Type 2 diabetes, apparently, being an occupational hazard for the travelling salesman). "Everything here is handmade," he says. "You know they are never going to stiff you. That's important. It's the same way I do things. When I sell someone something, nobody ever asks me the price. I'm not out to screw them. They know that."

Back in the car Steve takes out his recorder and repeats, "Disinfectant, dish soap, paper towels and floor cleaner." The order from Gigi's Café is run-of-the-mill stuff for someone who, when called upon, is capable of so much more. A few weeks back, when a service station up the line needed a baby change table for its washroom, Steve found one. Not too long ago a surveyor in Shawville was burned out in a fire. One day Steve just showed up at his new office with a desk, chair, filing cabinets and assorted other office equipment, along with a couple of strong lads to install it. "One-stop shopping," Steve calls it.

You read a lot these days about customer loyalty being dead. Watching Steve makes a person think that's not necessarily the case. "On this job you meet a lot of people and make a lot of friendships," he says. "I'd say about 98 percent of my customers like me and the other two don't. I can live with that." Steve may look like a mere order taker, but that's missing his subtle art. Building relationships is what sales is all about. He keeps customers with the small things: if a customer mentions how he likes those little pens he gives away, Steve makes sure he drops a couple off next time he's passing. If someone has a question about how a cleaner works, he hustles over, rolls up his sleeves and shows them. No one, after all, reads directions anymore; they ask questions. When a store owner asks whether he can use this new toilet bowl cleaner in his septic tank, Steve had better know what the answer is.

Steve builds in lots of face time with customers—just appearing at the door for no particular reason other than to ensure they have everything they need. But he makes it a point not to tell a customer everything about a product. "Just give the highlights. Always keep something in reserve," he says. "I used to sell these shirts that had a double stay in the collar. That mattered because some competitors didn't have stays in their collars, which meant that they got all wrinkly. I didn't tell my customers why ours were better. I wanted to keep their interest. I wanted to keep them asking questions." As much as anything, he perseveres: last year he went to see a customer every week even though she bought nothing from him. After a year of visits he finally closed a sale.

Not that he ever pressures. "Don't try to sell someone on a Friday," he says when I ask about his rules for sales success. What he means is that at that point in the week, any self-respecting resident of the Pontiac is thinking about getting their power boat out on the lake, not whether they need more fax toner. Wait until Monday, on the other hand, and the business is yours.

We keep moving. On to a big family-owned épicerie, where Jean-Paul Béland, the proprietor and patriarch, unloads a beer truck in the parking lot. Inside, amid the rows of cheese and the freezers full of Salisbury steaks and peaches-and-cream corn, the first person Steve runs into is a young woman named Francis, whom Steve, for some reason, calls "Sparky."

"Hey, Steve, we need a new calculator. Can ours be fixed?"

"A Canon P-23?"

"Yep. The paper won't go through."

"I'll bring it this week," he says.

Then back in the van and across town to another grocery store. In a second-floor office Raymond and Robbie—two sturdy fellows in their thirties who look like they should be in buckskins out fording a river somewhere—peer glumly into the screens of desktop computers. Steve's arrival lightens their mood. For a few minutes they kibitz about something called "Bikes in the Bay," which turns out to be the local motorcycle festival. Somewhere in the conversation Steve reminds them that if they want their regular ad in the *Equity*'s Pontiac Travel Guide they will have to commit soon. For good measure he hits them up for thirty dozen hamburger patties and twenty dozen hot dogs for the *Equity*'s annual summer picnic.

Steve's exit route takes him down some back stairs and through the butcher shop, where a thick-bodied guy in a hard hat and blood-smeared white coat hacks at meat. Half-assed insults are exchanged: nobody is getting better looking or, from the sounds of it, any thinner. When Steve tells him about the store's picnic commitment, the butcher, whose name turns out to be Rennie, writes on a chalkboard: "Steve, 30 dozen patties, 20 dozen hot dogs June 30 The Equity."

Steve pulls up in front of the local youth employment centre. "Sometimes I get an order here, but usually it's waiting on the fax machine for me back at the office," he says. Today they want two packets of 8½ x 14-inch printer paper. He sticks his head inside the office at the local elementary school ("Nothing today.") and a food bank in the same brick building ("I think we're good."). The two sisters who run Kluke Snack—a narrow, elongated old-style diner—want to do some business. Back in the car, he repeats their order into his recorder: a bottle of Merlin cleaner for their fryer and grills. It retails for $9.95.

Sales folks, it has been my personal experience, are inattentive drivers: they're always illegally texting, talking to a customer on Bluetooth or mentally calculating a commission. They're usually running late. Steve is different. He drives within the speed limit, with both hands on the wheel. As we drive, he talks. Not in a wearying oh-my-god-let's-not-leave-a-second-of-dead-air manner. He makes friends with the pauses. He keeps his eyes on the road, as befitting a man who has seen many things and whose abiding principle is "every day you go to work you never know what is going to happen."

Steve had options when he graduated from Woodroffe High School: he could have joined the Mounties or the fire department. Instead, he opted for Art Forbes Enterprises, which his father formed after retail giant Dylex took over John Forsyth Shirts and axed the sales staff. Steve spent the next fifteen years selling Bench Craft leather belts from Kitchener, Ontario, along with trousers made by Rothstein Pants, and swimsuits, robes and pyjamas made by Majestic Industries, both of Montreal.

He and Art travelled together in his father's big Buick Estate wagon, then an Electra 225, finally a Pontiac Parisienne. They threw their samples into grips. They placed the bulky suitcases in the trunk—unlike a lot of travelling salesmen, who took out the back seat of the car and replaced it with a piece of plywood for storing samples—and then hit the road. Through the hick towns of eastern Ontario and the mostly English townships of western Quebec they drove. In a cloud of spinning gravel, they'd wheel into places named Arnprior, Renfrew, Deep River, Pembroke, Brockville, Kingston and Belleville and hump their goods into men's stores that had stood there for generations. "[When I was] growing up, Father was away a lot," Steve says. "I hated the day he was leaving. But over the years we grew very close. We were more like brothers than father and son. When he died, I lost my best friend and my father in a single day."

Travelling with Art, Steve watched, listened and learned. From the age of twelve on Steve had been copying out and memorizing his dad's motto: "Good, better, best: I will never rest till my good is better and my better best." As they worked together, Art taught him other things: "The customer isn't always number one," for starters. But also that "if a customer has more than three sock companies on the rack, you will have only trouble getting paid," since the store owner clearly can't say no to a salesman even if they don't really think they can move the merchandise. He counselled Steve to trust his own judgment when deciding what merchandise to show customers. ("You may have a shirt in fifty colours and stripe combinations. Pick out the ones you like. Show them to the customer and you'll build a trust and rapport with them.") Some of things he urged were self-evident: "Don't ever slam a door, because you never know when it will open again" and "Don't try to sell your product by talking down the competition." When he told Steve to "always be closing," his father meant that you need to be always closing in on the next step in the sales process.

Art knew the dangers of overselling. Every Christmas he sent blocks of Black Diamond cheddar cheese to their customers. He never sent booze for the simple reason that if a bottle of Canadian Club rye arrived at a customer's place of business, it would almost never make it to their home unopened. The customer, instead, would arrive half in the bag and late on Christmas Eve. The wife would blame it on Art Forbes and Associates. Next thing you knew a competitor would have the business.

Together Art and Steve spent fifty weeks a year on the road, taking orders, prospecting for new clients and keeping existing accounts happy. "I was in town," Steve would say to customers when he finally got on his own, "and I just wanted to drop in because I had few things I thought you would like to see." Like his father before him, he would unsnap his grip and, as if unveiling a saint's relics, drape a shirt or tie over his arm for the owner's discerning gaze. Orders would be scribbled down for transcription back at the office. Then, on to the next customer, often a few miles down the highway.

Sometimes clients would come into the office in Ottawa to see samples. The Forbes boys would set up booths at trade shows. A few times a year they made their way across town to sell to the procurement guy who supplied the Canadian forces bases in Canada, Bermuda and West Germany. Spring, fall and late summer Steve and Art packed up their grips and boarded a plane for the Caribbean. They checked into the Elbow Beach Surf Club in Bermuda—where the seventies potboiler *The Deep* was filmed—or the Astra Suites in Barbados or the Grand Bahama Hotel on Grand Bahama Island. Sometimes they had a sample room where they could put their clothes on display. Mostly they visited clients: Leo Custodio and Charles Dickens in Bermuda, Michael Lambert in Barbados and Pat Paul in Nassau. "I used to try and get all business done in the first couple of days," Steve recalls. "I would get there on Tuesday and make appointments for Wednesday. Then Thursday, Friday and Saturday you could put your grips away and relax." Some 45 percent of their annual sales came from the islands. When their Caribbean customers travelled to Canada, the Forbes boys ensured that they stayed at the stately Rothstein residence in Mount Royal and received a tour of the factories that made the merchandise they sold in their stores.

For fifteen years they worked together. When Art retired in 1988, Steve discovered that the business was changing. All of a sudden the big manufacturers like Dylex were charging for samples: on a four-thousand-dollar commission Steve had to cough up five figures for the shirts, pants, underwear, jackets and ties that were his main sales props. No such concerns weighed on him in the job he took next: selling Wonder Bras throughout the Ottawa Valley. "In sales you sell yourself," says

Steve. "Bras are a different product that ties and belts. But in the end it is just the same thing."

Steve would leave on Sunday night and return on Friday. He would spend Saturday checking invoices. Then on Sunday he would do it all again. He was only forty, but had spent too many of those years on the road and was sick of so much time alone in motels, eating heart-stopping poutine and watching the Canadiens play on fuzzy TV screens. He took a job that allowed him to finish each day at home near Ottawa: selling towels, linens, toilet paper, garbage bags and floor stripper to motels along the St. Lawrence Seaway. When that outfit was taken over, Steve found work selling chemicals and, later, a job in Quebec's Pontiac County, where the Forbes clan had long owned a cottage, peddling office products. For fourteen years he commuted back and forth to Ottawa. Then he met Anne. By the time Steve's employer got in trouble and had to lay him off the Pontiac had become home. He says, "I left that job on a Friday. On Tuesday I started work at the *Equity*."

THERE'S not a lot of customer turnover in the Pontiac. People tend to be lifers who've never left or retirees uninterested in opening up a business in a small, rural market. Steve sells all things to all customers because there's no other way to make a buck in the work he has chosen in the place he wants to be. Consequently one minute he's talking stationery with the suits at the local insurance company or fax paper with the receptionist at a doctor's office and the next he's stepping inside the CPM Service Station where the regulars have assembled:

John Lunam, known as "McGill" because that's where he attended university; "Doc" Chrétien, a dentist; "NASCAR," the racing buff; and Noel, "the Mechanic," who, naturally, owns the place.

Once a week they convene there at noon and eat lunch around the wood stove at the back of the service station. It's one of those male environments where the ritual of a well-turned insult is more valued than expressing "one's feelings." Steve sits down, puts his feet up and lets the minutes tick by. Technically it's work, since he sells Noel various cleaners, fluids and other stuff. Yet I get the undeniable impression that Steve would do what he does—the daily rounds, the schmoozing and the passing of gossip—free. He is a travelling salesman in the age of Amazon and eBay. For now, he's like those old-time peddlers, the chime of bells heralding their eternally optimistic arrival over the hilltop.

In Ladysmith—home to Catholic Irish and Lutheran Germans—we lunch at a customer's bar in the town's sole hotel. Then we light out cross-country for Bristol, his home-town, and the metal hangar that houses Bristol Marine, a boat repair shop. The proprietor, Brent Orr, is tall and wide, with alert blue eyes and white hair bisected with a neat side part. Since Brent also happens to be Bristol's mayor, they talk municipal politics for a couple of minutes. His Worship doesn't need any hand cleaner, toilet paper, paper towels or stationery today. So Steve is soon on his way, heading back past Shawville to Quyon, a little port on the Ottawa River.

We drive around for a bit, taking in the ferry, the fabled Shamrock Bar at Gavan's Hotel and some of the other sites, until we park across the street from a stone Anglican Church.

"I want you to meet someone," he tells me, getting out and walking back down Clarendon Street. "Hellooo, Mae," Steve says. A straight-backed woman with a tight head of white curls, glasses and an apron says hi but keeps moving. Mae McCann, seventy-five, has been serving poutine, burgers, hot dogs, egg rolls and fries on that spot since 1969. "He's a good lad," she says of Steve, who has been supplying her with grill cleaner, bill pads, calculator rolls, disinfectant, paper towels and toilet paper for more years than he can say. "You can count on him."

It's three-ish as we head back toward Shawville, so what the heck: Steve cuts the wheel and crunches gravel up the long driveway to R.H. Nugent Equipment Rentals, where Paul Nugent—in his blue M. Willett ball hat and blue Adidas T-shirt—steps out from the back. They are men so the level of discourse is low: a little scandalous chitchat, girls, insults about Paul's fishing abilities and Steve's waistline. The conversation just flows naturally along.

Eventually things run their course. Steve asks, "Need anything, Nuge?" And Nuge, who depends upon him for toner cartridges, floor, glass and hand cleaner, paper towels and stationery supplies, replies, "No—I'm good, buddy." Steve is fifty-six and has never done anything other than a job that may be dying out. If his face registers a flicker of disappointment, it happens too quickly for me to see. Salesmen sell. Tomorrow he's in cottage country. He'll have a clean order book. The weather is supposed to be gorgeous.

CHAPTER
NINE

SHOTIME

Check one, check one. Niner, niner . . . I know the equipment works.
I just always wanted to be a roadie. That guy at the concert who came
on for about thirty minutes going "check, check." You could time your
buzz to that guy. Yep, my career goal was to be a roadie, and if you
look around you can see I didn't overshoot by much.

PAUL Peterson—the owner, operator and chief projectionist
at the Mustang Drive-in on County Road 1 just outside of
Picton, Ontario—has been emceeing the nightly show here for
eighteen years. When he figures enough cars have arrived, he
mutters, "Is it dark enough? Well, let's start it then." He flicks
the switch on the radio transmitter. The vintage rock stops.
He begins to talk. The words seep from a hundred car radios,

rising above the seam of land and sky before evaporating into the gloaming. Some people say Paul's sneaky way of starting the show is their favourite part of the whole evening. He begs to disagree. All the same, when he opens his mouth to ask the price of a head of lettuce in a grocery store checkout line, complete strangers turn, stare and ask if he is the "drive-in movie guy."

Speaking of natural segues: Hello, my name is Paul. I'll be your owner tonight. Thanks for coming. You know there are a lot of things I love about my job—the movies, the people, the charging you to get in. Oh yeaaaaaah, that works really well. Seriously, while I am ethically challenged and most people think I'm so crooked I could hide behind a corkscrew, if you have fun tonight, tell someone else. We've built this business on word of mouth. No one believes anything I say, but if you tell them, they listen. By the way if you don't have fun, keep it to yourself. Nobody likes a whiner.

The heavens have been opening and closing all day in southwestern Ontario. But the show at the Mustang goes on rain or shine; people know that when they buy their tickets. Tonight—seventeen degrees with not a single cloud or mosquito in the sky—they're offering the real goods: *Date Night* and *The A-Team* on the bigger front screen, *Shrek 2* and *Iron Man 2* on the smaller, more family-oriented back screen. Usually five hundred or so customers turn up for first-run movies on a Saturday night during the summer. With lousy weather looming, tonight's gate is just 217. The Mustang's grounds roil with life anyway: toddlers in pyjamas wriggle on the slides and swings; families open up the backs of their vans for a panoramic view of the big screen; couples slap on bug spray and snap open lawn chairs. Cars full of teens—giddy with the prospect of some serious dry-humping—traverse the hard-packed dirt and grass toward the rows of speakers. Beefy women in capris and middle-aged men with swollen prostates make a last dash for the washroom. Children, eyes startled with wonder, burst into the canteen and halt dead in their tracks.

A few things you need to know: If you have daytime running lights, congratulations, you have a nicer sled then me. I've never owned a vehicle from the decade I was living in, but hey, I'm not bitter. Here's the thing. If you do turn your car off, put the emergency brake on and then restart it. That will normally work and you won't light up the night sky or the car in front of you. If you need a boost, come and see me and I'll get you on your way. I have cables a battery pack and an old copy of Popular Mechanics. *We haven't lost a car yet. If the canteen is closed, you'll find me slipping into something more comfortable, like a coma, in the crappy van at the front of the canteen. Our website is* thechequesinthemail.com. *Go there, sign the guest book, and you can subscribe to our weekly newsletter. We then sell that list to a guy who sells life insurance for Amway.*

Paul greets them all from behind John Lennon glasses that glow lunar white from the movie screen half a football field away. "My parents always told me that Jerry Garcia didn't die," a woman who goes by the handle "Lover Grrl" wrote in the Mustang's online guest book, "he just owns the drive-in." Paul has a face built for Woodstock: his deep-socketed, gentle eyes and wide wedge of nose framed by salt-and-pepper beard, and shoulder-length hair that looks like it was carved from steel wool. The voice is contemplative, a little world-weary; the wisest guy at the best used-vinyl shop in town. Things are "cool," "great" or "terrific." Paul is prone to verbal shrugs: everybody else is "smart," "good" and "reliable." At best, he's just "lucky."

A tad under six feet, with some extra weight around the middle, he ambles around in a black turtleneck, cargo shorts and sandals. I say "ambles" because he's a big guy. But also because he doesn't seem to fret or worry enough to get his pulse rate over eighty. Paul is a businessman. When he looks out the window tonight, he must see dollar bills sprouting wings and taking flight as though part of the retro cartoon he is showing on the big screen. By rights he should be stomping his feet. He should be shaking a fist to the heavens and, eyes bugging out of his head, cursing like Yosemite Sam. Instead, he leans into the transmitter and informs the clientele that here at the Mustang Drive-in just buying a ticket doesn't ensure you see a movie.

If you've been here before, you know that this is the audience participation portion of tonight's show. Sometime during the Paleolithic period . . . Okay I'll skip ahead: about fourteen years ago we were making the jump to radio sound and it wasn't exactly a seamless transition, and one night in a moment of desperation or inspiration I came on the mike and said, "Look, you're going to honk at some point tonight, so why don't we just get it out of the way right now." Honk your horns, folks. Remind the neighbours how great it is to live next to a drive-in, and don't suck or I'll come back on the mike and mock you.

The din rises. Paul waits about a minute, then asks his pigtailed granddaughter, Anna, if it's loud enough. When a nine-year-old thumb goes up, Paul flicks the transmitter switch. The big projector begins to hum. The blandly handsome faces of Steve Carrell and Tina Fey fill the screen. No one would suggest *Date Night* is destined for "The Criterion Collection." And Paul has got a million things he should be doing. But the film only arrived a day ago and moving pictures just seem to draw his eye. They always have. So, he stands transfixed, peering through the little projector window. Watching the giant image of a man who appears to be trying to expunge his spleen through his nose, as the moon smoulders overhead.

THE Mustang Drive-in opened in April of 1956. A month later Paul, the son of a homemaker and a restless dairyman-turned-army-engineer, came into the world. So there's a certain karmic inevitability that, thirty-two years later, he and his wife, Nancy, would be tooling around aimlessly one day just outside of Picton and notice a For Sale sign in front of the Mustang. It would have taken special people to sense the potential back then. Paul wouldn't have known the backstory: how in 1932 Richard M. Hollingshead Jr.—the sales manager for the New Jersey–based Whiz Auto Products—thought it would be a good idea to nail a white sheet to two trees, place a radio behind the makeshift screen and then mount a Kodak movie projector on the hood of his car. How out of that deluded-sounding scheme sprang the "open-air theatre" or "ozone," which, in time, came to embody every nostalgic impulse ever felt by a North American baby boomer. How the Mustang began as part of a chain created during those heady times. And how, by 1988, the drive-in was fading to black owing to the ascent of the VCR and cable TV and the urban sprawl swallowing up the land where outdoor screens once flickered.

It helped that Paul didn't grow up thinking about profit margins and business plans. A dreamy, imaginative boy, by grade six he was in a band playing Tommy James and the Shondells covers ("Crrimmsssooonn and Cloooover, ooover and ooover"). Going all love-peace-marijuana-kill the pigs was not encouraged in the Peterson household. Paul caught the counterculture bug anyway, becoming the guy with the stack of *Mad* magazines under his bed and the milk crate full of psychedelic vinyl in the corner. The cool dude trying to sell his buddies on Monty Python, *A Clockwork Orange* and *O, Lucky Man!* (he loved Alan Price's soundtrack) when everyone else was watching *Dirty Harry* and *Summer of '42*.

Naturally he was drawn to lost causes. When it came time to choose a profession, he decided to help kids in crisis. Paul worked at a youth treatment centre in Richmond, British Columbia, and with street gangs in Vancouver. Later he returned to Ontario to toil for the Kingston Children's Aid Society as a residential care worker for children in crisis. (At one point, he lost most of his hair and all of his eyebrows after opening the door to a resident's room as she ignited the discharge of an aerosol can with a lighter.) He worked with the victims of sexual abuse. Some of his clients were prone to self-mutilation.

During the heat wave of 1998, when Paul and Nancy drove up County Road 1 past fields of corn, beans and strawberries, they could have glanced at the rusty, overgrown

Mustang Drive-in, seen a forlorn symbol of a culture that had lost its way and continued driving. Instead, Paul pulled over, turned off the ignition and they got out. Paul took a couple of steps forward, gravel crunching under his feet. By then he was searching for a job that, end of day, would leave him with enough energy to put in a few hours working on his unpublished novels and screen and stage plays. Just looking at the Mustang jump-started fond memories of heading to the drive-in growing up in Kingston. And so he gazed up at the big screen and, in a voice rich with possibility, said the fateful words: "This could be cool."

Nancy, who then ran her own restaurant in addition to her Children's Aid Society duties, was skeptical. But drive-ins have an ability to make any adults of a certain age take leave of their senses. Something about remembering the subversive pleasure of being up late in your jammies while the other kids are home in bed, the economy of carload nights, the freedom of being able to make jokes at the screen while your parents smoked in the front seat. Growing up in the early sixties, even a Maritime kid with a brush cut and bad teeth could sense that strange days were upon us. To me the world still seemed orderly and familiar amid those rows of chrome and steel, speakers strapped like umbilical cords to the car windows, as I watched the dancing wiener on the big screen.

Half a century later, I'm living proof of the abiding pull that a drive-in movie screen has on the imagination. It would be easy to look at the twenty or so drive-ins currently operating in this country—accounting for less than a hundred full-time jobs the last time anyone bothered to look—and the estimated four hundred that have gone dark since the boom days in the late fifties and conclude that this is an industry on its last legs. Except every year nearly two million Canadians buy a ticket. If that's not staying power, I don't know what is.

I'm not the only person who thinks so. In 1998, photographer Carl Weese pulled his truck off the road in rural Connecticut. It took him a minute to figure out that he was looking at the screen of an abandoned movie theatre, overgrown with trees. A day later he got up early and photographed the screen at daybreak. He liked the result well enough to put it in a small travelling show of prints he was mounting.

What surprised him was that people reacted to the shot. "However they responded to the other pictures in the portfolio, everyone reacted to the print of the drive-in," he wrote in the commentary for his show *The American Drive-in Theater*, which includes some of the hundreds of drive-ins he has since photographed across the United States. "Some recognized the subject immediately. Others stared and stared before 'getting it.'" Once the subject was identified, a smile was the invariable response, and then often a dreamy look as long-forgotten memories resurfaced. It was a showstopper.

Having seen his photos, which make drive-ins look like ancient ruins, I'm not remotely surprised. Weese thinks the rural settings touch something within people. Even the abandoned old screens, he writes, "resonate with the spirit of all who had spent time at them." Mostly what tugs at the glaze-eyed folks who stand before Weese's photos is the desire to reconnect with the objects of youth. They, more than anything, are reminders that there was a time when not every waking hour was spent worrying about fibre intake and whether little Aidan can cut it in French immersion.

I think people also love drive-ins because they're reminded that people in this country once did lots of things together: they shopped at farmer's markets; they went to church; they caught ball games, vaudeville shows and political rallies. Much of this coming together occurred in itinerant venues like carnival midways and tents where revivalist preachers, Chautauqua performers and travelling snake oil salesmen performed. Some of what they watched once upon a time— glowering wrestlers, ready to pay prize money to anyone who could survive a few rounds—smacked of ancient Rome. Nonetheless, sitting together hoping your hockey team would slap the shit out of the squad from the neighbouring town forged communal identities. Most of us have experienced the wonder of being part of a group uplifted as one by a song or some ringing oratory. And research shows that people who get out of the house and interact with others in some way are not only happier but also live longer.

That, alas, is just not the way the universe is going. Churches are closing and service clubs disappearing. Concert crowds have dwindled to the point where it's hardly worth it for Mick Jagger to take his death rictus on tour. Video games, let alone video movies, outsell old-fashioned ass-in-the-seat cinema viewing. Anyone can see where this is inevitably headed: a society increasingly alienated from family, friends and neighbours; a species forgoing real human connection to sit at home in the eerie light of the computer screen, forming "meaningful" relationships online. A long time ago Yogi Berra declared, "If you don't go to someone's funeral, they won't go to yours." That pretty much sums it up for me. When I thought too much about the disconnected situation, I found my hand involuntarily reaching for the Lagavulin. Instead, I headed for the door to go find some real people. And that, in a roundabout way, was how I found myself at the Mustang.

⌒

WHEN Paul bought the Mustang, it looked like a place haunted by poltergeists: the single screen full of holes, the grounds a neglected grass lawn, the speakers mostly gone. The owners only booked old, B-list movies. The audience consisted mainly of bored local teenagers jazzed on Labatt Blue looking for a party. The first thing Paul did was to take out an ad in the *Picton Gazette* informing readers that the Mustang had a zero tolerance attitude toward alcohol on the premises. Overnight, business dropped from six hundred or seven hundred customers to just 150. Teens driving by on the highway heckled the new owners. Paul, who in a previous life worked with big-city street gangs, did a lot of the security himself. Sometimes it felt like he was a bouncer at some bucket of blood back in East Vancouver. He says, "It took a while to get the word out that the Mustang was a good, clean family place."

You approach the Mustang now the same way they did then: through lovely countryside untouched by the wineries, herb farms, antique shops and intuitive energy healing studios native to Ontario's Prince Edward County. The air tonight smells of birch, pine, dust, grass and distant thunderstorms. Beyond the fields and their utilitarian farmhouses loom woods known to hold coyote and wildcat. Arrive at the Mustang a few hours before the first carload, however, and the initial thought is deserted, not ominous. There's only one way in: past the beaten-up 70 mm movie projector and the scruffy little garden with the miniature ceramic pagoda, and beyond the wooden sign so worn that it is difficult to make out ("Your licence number has been recorded. If a headset has been taken from the place you were parked, you will be contacted by the O[ntario] P[rovincial]P[olice]—The management"). Until you come to the old city-of-Kingston bus that serves as the ticket booth.

Things from here on in seem a little dreamy, a feeling exaggerated by the first objects visible inside the grounds: an aged fire truck; a vintage Coke machine; a retro Yamaha bike; rows of old speaker posts still standing like sentinels, even though the audio comes in on the car radio. Five years ago Paul opened up the wallet to replace the main screen. (It used to be maintained by men in chairs, anchored to a truck, who swung from side to side as they worked their way to the ground. Now he brings in a bucket truck, climbs in and makes the repairs himself.) Tradition had it that drive-in owners, to save a little money, used to live in an apartment within the A-framed screen. There's nothing livable about the Mustang's new forty-eight-foot-by-thirty-foot steel-and-plywood screen. Opening a door into its bowels, I look upward and, once my eyes have adjusted to the gloom, see metal crossbeams and dive-bombing swallows. Shafts of light, entering through ragged holes, crisscross. The ground is covered with debris—old reels and popcorn makers, Recommended as Adult Entertainment signs. The air is heavy and stagnant.

The screen out back is smaller. Thanks to the drive-in's oddball business model, it is also more lucrative. Of the $10 ticket price, $1.50 goes to government taxes. Roughly $5.10 on a first-run movie like *The A-Team* or *Date Night* goes to the film company. Studios, in fact, go to great lengths to assure they are getting their rightful cut; whenever someone new starts showing up regularly at the Mustang, Paul's first thought is "movie company flunky" checking to see whether he is underreporting the box office take. In any event, that leaves roughly $3.40 for the house.

The caveat is that the film company's take declines—and the owner's margins increases—the longer a movie is shown. *Shrek 2,* which had been out for nearly a month by the time of my visit, only nets 35 percent for the film company versus 60 to 70 percent in week one. Paul's strategy, therefore, is clear: bring in first-run, big-name flicks on the big screen. Then, after a couple of weeks move them onto Screen 2, where they can have a good long run, and sort of watch the dough roll in. "The second screen paid for itself halfway through the first season," Paul says. *Shrek 2,* for example, is still drawing them in. "The only thing close I can think of is *Anaconda.* People loved that movie. It was so cheesy. But people still showed up several times. That's pretty cool."

It's also a canny business tactic. The drive-in movie industry, the story goes, is run by sentimental throwbacks who just can't let go of the family business, even if it doesn't make a lick of commercial sense. Paul's laid-back sensibility seems to hide some hard-headed commercial instincts. Recently he and Nancy closed one of the two indoor theatres they own in the area. The cash flow from the Mustang and the Boulevard Cinema, the theatre they own in nearby Napanee, are helping to fund the acquisition of another indoor movie house by their daughter Hollie and one being built by their son Jamie.

Paul, at this moment, is fiddling with some machinery

inside the Screen I projectionist's booth: grey floors covered with old reels, tool boxes and rectangular film cases; clashing green and white walls bearing switches labelled with masking tape ("exciter lamp," "supply pre-amp," "moving volume") and a wooden sign that reads "Mustang Drive-In home of the triple feature." The gear—big projectors, crinkly silver air conditioning pipe—emits a vaguely dystopian aesthetic. It smells like machine oil, solvent and popcorn in here. In other words, it is just as you imagined it.

Within the booth, Paul explains, things have changed. Generally, though, the basics of showing films are the same as they've always been: films still travel in large cases consisting of about seven or eight reels. The reels each hold about twenty minutes of film. Paul used to use two projectors: as reel one was ending, he'd start reel two on the second machine. As reel two was playing, he would then load the third reel on the first projector. And so on and so on.

Time was when the ways a projectionist could screw up were myriad. There were blackouts. The highly flammable film burst into flame if it stalled in front of the ultra-hot carbon arc lamp. Projectionists put reels in backward, or in the wrong order. (Although during long, boring films entire reels were sometimes mysteriously left out with no one in the audience the wiser.) If the transitions were sloppy, the audience would let you know. Being an old-time projectionist had other hazards too. A lot of the carbon arc lamp houses weren't properly ventilated. Those exhaust fumes were toxic.

Now, using a small X-Acto knife, Paul simply splices the reels together into one giant reel—an average-length movie like *Date Night* uses about a mile of film—that is wound around a rotating table called a "platter." The film is then fed vertically into the top of his Xetron projector. Gear-like wheels pull the film frame by frame through the projector. Instead of carbon arc lamps, Paul's projectors now use 3,000-watt bulbs containing xenon gas, which are positioned in front of a reflective parabolic mirror. Without the shutter—a small propeller-like device that rotates twenty-four times a second—everything would flicker or look out of focus. Instead, when the image appears on the screen, it looks true to life, magical.

The new platter system is automatic. But not perfect: if the projector jams or the shutter is left open, the film will still burn, although only a single frame of it. Some lousy splicing, leaving the picture out of focus, and the crowd screams for the projectionist's head. A screw-up of any sort means you're off-screen for a minimum of twenty minutes. That's often enough for car engines to bark to life and customers to make for the exits.

Over the clamour of the movie audio, the projector motor and the air conditioning, Paul says that adding another screen would help pad profit margins. That's just not who they are. If money was the be-all and end-all, he and Nancy would have stayed with the industry-wide practice of playing the night's big feature film last to keep customers on the premises and spending as long as possible. Instead, he leads with the big-ticket item, so that families can enjoy it and still get the kids home to bed on time.

The real money isn't at the ticket booth anyway. Paul tells me the secret: every person who buys a ten-dollar ticket spends another twenty dollars on grub. A good night at the canteen takes in about $4,500. To gross that amount Paul spends about $1,500, which means that he nets about $3,000—a Warren Buffett-like 200 percent return on his nightly investment. "Movies are a popcorn delivery system," he says. "The markups are so huge." When I ask precisely how huge, he snickers and says that he would tell me, but then he would have to kill me to keep the secret. The most he will say is that the bag costs more than the popcorn inside it. Then he adds, "Oh yeah, did I say that nachos are a beautiful thing?"

He leads the way into the canteen—ten feet by twenty-five feet, festooned with movie posters. It is manned by his wife, Nancy, slim with reddish hair, and a pleasant young woman wearing a badge that says Charlene. The canteen is also a beautiful thing: the noir-ish glow of the slushies, the grandeur of the popcorn machine—where, nightly, sixty pounds of kernels along with special seasoning and canola oil are popped into bright yellow perfection—the possibility of the deep-fat fryer from which emerge French fries, onion rings, hamburgers, hot dogs and Pogos. A few feet away plastic containers full of onions, hot peppers, ketchup and relish await ladling. I ogle the kind of crap I haven't eaten since I was a kid: Ring and Push Pops, Drumsticks, Pixy Stix, radioactive-looking cotton candy. My eye lands on stuff I've never seen at a movie house before—Nancy's homemade fudge, mosquito coils, Frisbees embossed with the kicking-horse Mustang logo.

It's the smell that really transports: frying fat, grease, cheese, onions and butter, or at least, something butter-like. The feeling it conjures is the bovine thrill that goes with the knowledge that when these smells waft through my nasal passages, something absolutely wonderful will follow. Somewhere in a back copy of the *New England Journal of Medicine* there could be a study concluding that people like to eat food laden with enough trans fats to stop a bull moose because it stimulates something deep in the brain stem. I just don't want to know. Examining some things too closely plain drains the fun right out of them.

Okay folks, we'll be back on-screen in ten minutes and in the mean-time I'll fire up some white screen for the kids if they want to try their hand at shadow puppets And let me remind you that there's no point in taking any money home with you, so come on in and buy stuff. If you're leaving, drive safely—if you're staying, park safely—and I think you all know what that means. Canteen will close in ten.

There are two intermissions—one for each screen—at the Mustang. Back in the early days the teens would come staggering from their cars, looking for something, anything, to absorb the booze. Tonight kids in pyjamas and carrying blankets line up behind teenagers, all flushed and glassy eyed from a couple of hours pressed together in an airless vehicle. Paul doesn't judge. He just stands in the doorway, working the room without actually moving, the trace of a grin on his face even when he's not actually smiling.

Often it's the sight of a familiar face. Like a black-shirted Crown attorney from a nearby town named Paul who saunters over along with his wife, a photographer named Anita. A woman named Amanda waves. A guy who summers in the area—and who once sought out Paul's advice on his marital woes—tells him confidentially that the union is back on the rails. A Celt named Angus, hands full of canteen fare, makes a detour to pay his respects. A couple of college students from Ottawa, there in a Smart car, want to know if they can sleep under a picnic table if they're too tired to make the two-hundred-kilometre drive home.

Paul speaks to everyone like they went to kindergarten together. "People just like to check in," he says. "Sometimes I feel like a Wal-Mart greeter. But I've made some terrific friends." The repeat business—the vacationers who summer in the Picton area and the locals coming since they were little shavers—speaks to that. Tammy, who has been working at the Mustang for twenty-one years, and Grace, with fifteen years of service, are more friends than paid employees. Some of his pals just show up and work free: Paul, the aforementioned lawyer, has been helping out since having to run interference for his namesake with angry patrons complaining about the lousy sound quality. His wife, who almost always ends up helping in the kitchen, has seen more customers than movies.

To some, the owner seems to enjoy a status far more rarefied than that of a humble movie projectionist. Five years ago, when a couple of regulars named Dale and Darla got hitched at the Mustang, Paul officiated. One Halloween he did the honours at another on-site wedding as a personal favour to another regular—a high school adolescent-care worker as well as one of the stars of a reality TV show called *Outlaw Bikers*.

Before visiting the Mustang, I went online and clicked on the guest book to try to get a sense of what it is that people like so much about the experience. For some it was predictably the bittersweet journey to a nicer, better time: "Our 39th Anniversary is Jan. 30, 2010," writes Susie, "and when we were younger with 3 boys we used to pack them up and put them in our 1966 Oldsmobile and bring them here to watch the movies."

"Some of my fondest memories are from my first summer job working at the drive-in, 1971 when i stayed with my aunt and uncle who ran it then," writes Dogbytes. "Along with my cousins, I was part of the grounds and snack bar crew, and I learned to splice film, run the projector and re-wire torn off speakers . . . all great fun for a lad of 12."

Tidrock1 just wanted to thank Paul "for bringing back all those warm, childlike feelings that i have not felt in so many years! If it was not for people like you an era gone long ago, an era of fun and youthfulness would be lost forever, please keep up the outstanding work, and let's keep this ultimate form of movie going alive!!!!"

Some people dig the tunes ("Thanks for playing Bruce Springsteen all the time.") and the grub ("Every weekend we are there watching movies in the middle row with my buttered popcorn and her French Fries. I don't know what I would do with my summers if something happened to this place."). Some seem to be actually there for the movies. ("During the winter months, we watch vintage drive-in intermission videos and count the days to spring and more Mustang memories," one couple wrote.)

Paul is mighty grateful for everyone's support. He gives shout-outs over the loudspeaker to birthday celebrants. He happily shares the nuances of the projectionist's trade with anyone who walks in the door. He answers emails. He writes a semi-regular blog about his movie likes and hates—a spinoff from the movie reviews he does for a trio of Ontario newspapers. (FYI: his all-time favourite flick is *American Beauty,* with

The Verdict, Three Days of the Condor, the *Godfather* trilogy and *Apocalypse Now* close behind.)

At one point during my visit Paul indicated two trees at the front of the property. One is dedicated to the late Katie Graszat, a teacher who volunteered at the Mustang more than she ever watched movies. The other tree is in memory of a young man named Jay Hoskins, another volunteer, who died in a car accident. He and his girlfriend used to come to the Mustang three or four times a week. Eventually Paul just said the hell with it and gave them a permanent free pass.

Paul, it must be said, seems to genuinely like the human race. Which may explain why he hasn't entirely left his past life as a youth crisis worker behind. He's written a book—and an accompanying interactive application—that follows four survivors of near-fatal suicide and asks the question: what if those who succeeded in taking their own lives had waited a day? He still gets calls from old clients. One is a woman in her early thirties who was horribly abused from the ages of four to seventeen. Somewhere along the line she was diagnosed with multiple personality disorder, an ailment that many specialists think is bogus. "My attitude is: whatever it takes you get through your pain," Paul says.

Thirteen years ago she showed up at the drive-in and told him that she was going to kill herself. The two of them walked around the drive-in grounds for hours. Throughout, several different personalities surfaced. Paul talked to all of them before finally convincing her to check into a hospital. Today she's a happy mother of five. Sometimes she takes her kids to the Mustang to watch the movies and catch up with her old counsellor.

The drive-in business, Paul likes to say, has turned out to be a really good way to make hours and entire days disappear. Running a drive-in may sound pretty idyllic to a sixteen-hour-a-day dairy farmer or an eighty-hour-a-week downtown lawyer. But the past five years he and Nancy have cancelled exactly two shows during their eighteen-week season—because of weather. They run four movies on All-Nighter Night. On P.J. Night, when every kid wearing jammies gets in free, the gate can swell to 550 paying customers. Usually Paul turns out the lights by 1:15. On Saturday evenings—Triple Feature Night—the last person doesn't leave until 4 a.m.

No wonder, during drive-in season, Paul and Nancy forgo their farmhouse for the apartment over the projection room. During the day there are toilets to unclog, speakers to rewire and popcorn machines to fix. ("I didn't start out doing stuff," Paul says, "but picked it up as I went along because I had to. My job is a little bit of everything, whatever it takes.") Whatever else is going on, come 6 p.m. Paul has to start rewinding the previous day's movies. He threads the film through the projector, He looks outside to see how many cars have arrived. Because, baby, it's showtime.

⌣

PAUL may move slowly around his domain, but after a while you notice that he is seldom at rest. He makes his rounds: sticking his head inside the none-too-pretty bathroom, checking on the projectors, strolling around the grounds. Come daylight he might find wallets, the occasional hooch bottle, even an iPod or two lying in the grass. "I find lots of unpleasant things too," he says, then adds, "It's good that people are doing things safely." Sometimes he wakes people up in various states of undress. Last season, as he approached a car, he was startled to see two naked females exit, open the back seats and then sprint the two feet to the front seat, slamming the doors behind them.

Generally, though, things are tame. It's been years since he's slapped a hammerlock on a high school senior crazy on Canadian Club. When he's satisfied that everything's under control, he takes Anna by the hand and they head up the stairs to watch some *Shrek 2* from the back-screen projection booth. At 11:50 p.m., when the first cars are starting up their engines, Paul is already in the kitchen, helping Nancy clean up. By his estimation, the rain cost him about three thousand dollars at the gate and canteen tonight.

He can't afford too many more nights like that. Margins are thin in this business. A few days of rain is a drag. A week is a catastrophe. But time moves slowly at this point in the evening. Paul is fifty-four years old; after a full day in a long week the bedroll beckons. He daydreams about getting out on his motorbike on the highway, and about what the season ahead will hold for his beloved New England Patriots. Sometimes he thinks about the moment he and Nancy shut the theatre for the winter, hop in their RV and join the caravan to Florida.

At 12:45 the credits roll down the big screen and Paul flips on the transmitter:

Tha . . . tha . . . tha . . . as Porky Pig used to say. Well, that's our program, folks. Thanks for coming, thanks for leaving. I hope you had fun, and if not, you figure out why you stayed till the end. See you on the other side of next time. Good night.

Then, as the credits continue, he cranks the AC-DC, has a seat and waits. Some people return their radios. A sheepish-looking father, son in tow, appears at the door of the projectionist's room and asks if Paul has some jumper cables. Paul tells him not to sweat it. He just smiles, hoists his gear up and follows them to their car. It happens three more times, which is about par for the course. At least every engine turns over. No one has to be driven home.

By now all the cars are gone. Stars crowd the country sky. The air has a crunch like a Granny Smith. From where I stand, I can see the headlights disappearing into the night. It's a lonely image, really.

God knows where exactly they are going. And what precisely waits for them there. It's all out of Paul's hands. All he does is his thing: Show a few movies. Try to bring some people together to take their pleasure the old-fashioned way. It's a small dream, he knows. He'll tell you this too: we'll only miss it when it's gone.

CHAPTER
TEN

A TRICK OF THE LIGHT

CHRISTINE Curtis was a lazy youth and a dreamy, sleep-until-noon teen. So it still surprises her that when the alarm clock jangles, she does not snake out a hand and hit the snooze button for the extra five minutes in the sack. Instead, at 3:45 a.m. she punches the alarm into silence. She tosses off the covers. She swings a leg over the side of the bed. She pulls herself into the sitting position. She might run a hand through her hair, which is reddish and thick with cowlicks. She might rub her eyes, which are green. She might yawn and groan. But always, on muscles hardened by lots of time outdoors but not a single spinning class, she eventually rises. She throws on her sweatshirt and sticks her feet in an old pair of slippers lined with fleece.

After six years, Chris could do the walk with her eyes closed. Sometimes it seems like she actually does as she heads into the kitchen, where the coffee maker automatically whirred into action twenty minutes earlier. She pours a mug, through pinched eyes watches the steam rise, then pushes open the door and steps out beneath the big beam of light. This woman, who once missed a plane because she simply couldn't bring herself to run through the air terminal, gets to work. Because people are waiting.

While her eyes are still accustomed to the dark, Chris looks up at the cloud cover. She takes a few steps from the back porch to the Stevenson screen, a box containing thermometers, to get the temperature. Then she walks over to the seawall and looks out at the ocean. Dawson Island sits at the confluence of Gulf Channel and Orca Sound, on the central coast of British Columbia. The island is about 160 miles south of Prince Rupert and 250 miles northwest of Vancouver. The lighthouse faces west, toward Queen Charlotte Sound. She uses familiar landmarks to calculate visibility. She looks at the waves. About thirty yards from her residence she opens a porch door and enters a room that, mercifully, is only partly lit. Using abbreviations, she writes down in a lined ledger everything she has learned. She stretches her back. She sips her coffee.

At 4:40 she reaches for the lighthouse radio, which looks like an old telephone. She listens, waiting for her turn, as the radio operator in Prince Rupert collects the "weathers," beginning at the northern stations and moving south until it's Dawson Island's turn.

"Go ahead with your marine local, Dawson," the operator finally says.

Chris waits a beat, then replies, "Prince Rupert, Dawson. We have cloudy, one-five plus. Southwest two-zero, gusting two-five. Two-foot chop, low southwest. Over."

What this means is the sky is cloudy, but the visibility is great, one-five, or fifteen miles, being about as good as it gets. The winds are blowing to the southwest about twenty miles an hour with gusts of twenty-five. There is a two-foot chop on the ocean.

All useful stuff for the occupants of sailboats, float planes, commercial freighters and tandem kayaks that look for the information online and on the continuous marine broadcast on VHF. When the radio exchange ends, Chris looks at the clock. It is ten minutes before five now. Everyone else on the island—her husband, Rob; head keeper, Miles, and his wife, Janelle—is asleep. Chris, one of eighteen female light keepers on the west coast, is human. On a point of pride, she would never head back to bed in her and Rob's bungalow, with its sturdy plaster walls and *circa* 1950s design—which, to the knowing eye, is immediately recognizable as a keeper's house. Old-timers used to refuse to shut their eyes for even a few minutes during a shift. But, times have changed. On a lazy day Chris can catnap right up until her next report, in three hours' time. Then she's awake for the day.

Her main job is ensuring the Dawson light keeps shining. It's a heavy responsibility: the light has pretty well shone hour after hour, day after day, since 1898, when the tower was built as one of a half-dozen lighthouses erected to guide starry-eyed prospectors to the Klondike during the gold rush. The current light, the fourth on this site, was constructed in the early 1980s after high seas drove a huge log into the last tower, knocking it on its side. Now it sits atop a metal, twenty-foot skeleton on a concrete base. Dawson Island is some fifty acres of old-growth rainforest. Only three of British Columbia's twenty-seven staffed light stations are accessible by road. The light itself— along with the engine room building and the two keepers' homes—sits on a three-acre islet connected to the rest of the island by a thin natural causeway that can be submerged at high tide or during rough seas. "When that happens," Chris says in her flat Ontario way, "this place can seem a whole lot smaller."

Automation means keepers have little to do with the lights anymore. All the staffed stations on the British Columbia coast are automated, meaning that the navigation aids can function even if neither keeper is around. Technicians from the mainland change the bulbs, which are now about the size of her thumb, compared with about the size of a human head when she started as a keeper around fifteen years ago. "We really just do maintenance now," she says. "We check that it's rotating and flashing at the right frequency. We check that it's operating correctly. Once a month we shut it down and clean it." The cleaning used to take a day. Now it takes about ten minutes.

Foghorns, which went electric in the 1970s, are equally low maintenance. Most lights don't even bother with them anymore; Dawson Island's is one of only seven now operating in all of British Columbia. Chris keeps the fog detector lenses clean so that they can send out sensory beams. Otherwise, they operate by solar panels that don't need to be changed. If something is wrong, she calls the technicians. She's been on Dawson Island for eleven months a year for the past eight years. So far she has called the techs a grand total of four times. They come via a helicopter, which puts down on the landing pad at the far end of the islet. Supplies can come on the helicopter or on a Coast Guard workboat, which uses an aerial derrick or "highline" to move stuff back and forth to the island. Chris also uses the highline to launch the light's boat, which, other than the helicopter, is the only way on or off Dawson Island.

⌒

"I USED to be a banker," Chris says, snickering in a way that says, *Now look at me.* "I used to wear a power suit with shoulders big enough to land a search-and-rescue helicopter." Now she wears a different uniform: jeans with a hole in the right rear pocket, a plaid work shirt over a navy T-shirt, worn black army-surplus-style workboots, a ball cap with a faded-to-unreadable patch. She's forty-eight years old—medium height and build—with lines around the eyes to prove it. A face with a lot going on: freckles, pale colouring, a vertical scar beside her right eye courtesy of a street hockey game back in the Leaside area of Toronto where she grew up.

Life was comfortable for the daughter of a lawyer and a CBC Radio producer: a nice high school run devoid of major crisis, a business degree at the University of Toronto, then an MBA at the same institution. Chris got a job in finance. There was a marriage and, three years later at the age of twenty-eight, an amicable enough divorce. She met Rob, a paramedic, at the Horseshoe Tavern during a Stompin' Tom Connors concert. Not long after that, Chris signed on with a gold exploration company. She later left for a tech start-up, watched her equity soar, then plummet, after the dot-com bubble burst. Then, within the space of eighteen months, her father died in a car accident and her only brother was diagnosed with multiple sclerosis.

"I was thirty-five years old," she says. "Rob [by then her husband] was three years younger, but burned out from his work. We were looking for something new. Somehow someone got us thinking about light keeping, which sounded pretty romantic and pretty different than what we were both doing. We got the forms from the Public Service Commission. One night over a few too many glasses of wine we said what the hell."

Light keepers, to her relief, weren't your standard civil servants. Work that involves complete isolation for eleven months a year tends to attract old hippies, misty-eyed romantics, 'Nam War draft dodgers, painters looking for a little solitude, along with folks who want to be close to nature and far from the civilizing influences of big cities. Oh sure, the service on the West Coast had its share of misanthropes and nut cases: authoritarian types who insisted on dressing in military uniform, who wouldn't let their assistant keepers use the radio telephones and decreed that everyone in the light drop whatever they were doing and wave at the *Queen of the North* ferry whenever it passed by. In one lighthouse, during the 1960s, relations between keeper and assistant keeper grew strained enough to culminate in a report that noted, "Apparently there has been very little communication between them since the shooting incident some time back."

What Chris is trying to say is that they were forewarned about what the job does to a person. What's more, the dark days of light keeping in Canada were under way. They knew then that this probably wasn't a job with a long career arc. Yet for some reason all the bad stuff they'd heard—the isolation, the cabin fever, the food and drink that had to be coptered in from the mainland, the difficulty with raising kids on a rock in the Pacific—failed to dissuade them. "We were smitten with the idea," she said, "and that was that." In March of 1995 she got word that they were in.

Lighthouse keeping used to be a man's world. By the 1960s, a few now-legendary women had talked their way onto lights as part of a two-keeper rotation. By the last years of the twentieth century Charlotte Point, which sits at the extreme northwest end of Haida Gwaii, was one of only three lights with female keepers. The most remote of all British Columbia's northern lighthouses, it is one hundred nautical miles west of Prince Rupert and thirty nautical miles south of the Alaskan border. The light, which was established in 1913, was built to guard the Dixon Entrance, the disputed boundary between Canada and the United States. During the Second World War it was painted camouflage green and a radar station was built nearby to keep watch on the North Pacific. Frances Mills, the head keeper, had worked her way up from assistant keeper at two other lights. Tall, with prematurely white hair and eyes that laugh, she lived there with her husband, Mel, who had his thirty years in as a weapons tech with the Canadian navy. She was standing by the landing pad the day that Chris and Rob—their minds whirling with oh-God-what-were-we-thinking uncertainty—*whump-whumped* by helicopter toward the island.

We're outside now. Sun has broken through the clouds, sending weird beams of light onto the tower as Chris dabs a little white on some chipped paint. This, she tells me, is what she mostly does: keeping everything shipshape. It's as much for the keepers themselves as for the bosses back on the mainland.

When your world is virtually just a few acres of land and a few buildings, you can't just let things go. Keepers, by necessity, are self-starters: they grow and catch their own food; when something breaks, they fix it. When it's time for a little R and R, they entertain themselves in a place where boxed sets of *The Wire* are hard to come by.

Chris—who grows tomatoes, beans, peppers and herbs out behind the house and plays bridge in addition to the French horn—is well suited to it. So is Rob, who makes sculpture from driftwood and does the *New York Times* crossword every day online. Rob catches fish that Chris smokes. He also does a passable imitation of Relic, the character on the old *Beachcombers* television series.

～

BY now it is time to reveal something that you may already have guessed. There is, as far as I know, no Dawson Island lighthouse. It is my deepest belief that there is not a Dawson Island either—at least, not one off the West Coast. I'll concede that there may well exist a Christine Curtis and that she could exhibit some of the qualities my Chris Curtis would display if she didn't live in my mind in a nonexistent lighthouse on a made-up island. If so, this is entirely coincidental.

I wanted to talk to a keeper of a British Columbia light because only three provinces still have humans manning the switches. (One of them, New Brunswick, keeps a single manned light on Machias Seal Island in the Gulf of Maine so that Canada can claim sovereignty over it.) The keeper I contacted said come on over. Then one day she sent me an email advising me that the only way I could in fact step onto her light was with the approval of the Canadian Coast Guard, which administers what's left of this country's lighthouses. My request to the Coast Guard bounced around a few times before finally being denied. "We think you're probably going to write about the de-staffing of the lighthouses," a Coast Guard spokesman told me. Which was and wasn't true.

Admittedly lighthouses are a touchy subject for the feds, particularly in British Columbia, where public outrage twice forced the government to shelve plans to make keepers obsolete. But not letting a reporter talk to the last men and women who will do this work made me double-click on the Coast Guard website to ensure they hadn't, in the dead of night, vapourized every existing light and secreted the folks who manned them away into the bowels of the civil service with the promise of a nice pension as long as they spoke not a word about the whole matter. The keepers, as far as I know, are still there. But the way the government is keeping them from journalists' eyes makes me think not for much longer.

That causes my heart to sink. We all know that in the twenty-first century everyone and everything must pay their own way. And liability issues are liability issues. But lighthouses aren't just majestic and symbolic. They aren't just old. They are history, which is way different. The first lighthouse on record was the Pharos of Alexandria, built in about 280 BC to guide sailors into the great harbour of Alexandria. Considered one of the Seven Wonders of the Ancient World, it was, by all accounts, something to see. The Pharos reportedly used fire at night and a sun-reflecting mirror during the day. The whole thing, including the foundation, was thought to be

384 feet high, which, if true, makes it the tallest lighthouse in history and the highest building in the ancient world.

Its fame, therefore, spread: The British called a lighthouse a "pharos" until 1600. The Romans—who built more than thirty lighthouses throughout their provinces, including the 1,900-year-old Tower of Hercules still overlooking the Atlantic coast of Spain—memorialized the Pharos on their coins. Some of the lights built after the end of the so-called Dark Ages, when trade among ports on the Mediterranean and beyond blossomed, still stand today: the *circa* 1245 lighthouse at the tip of the Hook Peninsula, in County Wexford, Ireland. The 700-year-old Cordouan lighthouse, which stands near the mouth of the Gironde estuary in France. But it wasn't until the fifteenth century that lighthouses began to be installed offshore to warn seamen of hazards to their vessels along routes to the port cities. Author D. Alan Stevenson estimated that the number of lighthouses worldwide grew from about thirty-four in 1600 to around 175 by 1800.

The first lighthouse in Canada—the second on the entire coast of North America after Little Brewster Island in Boston Harbor—was built on Cape Breton Island in 1734 at the fortress of Louisbourg, the major landfall for France in the New World. No surprise there: eight years earlier, three hundred people died when a French transport ship ran aground a few miles east of the fortress. When completed, the Louisbourg light tower stood about seventy-five feet high. The first light was a circle of cod liver oil–fed wicks set in a copper ring mounted on cork floats. Its flame was visible for eighteen nautical miles, an impressive distance for those times. Not far from the base of the light was a small house containing room for oil storage and quarters for the light keeper. From 1733 until 1744, this was Jean Grenard dit Belair, a retired sergeant of the Compagnies franches de la marine, and Canada's first full-time light keeper.

⌒

"THERE'S something about the light tower itself," Elaine Graham—a real person—tells me over the telephone. "People are smitten with them. I think it's a real click magnet: everyone wants to take a photo. I guess it is romantic in a way. A light is the ultimate lifesaving symbol. It is an expression of compassion." She says these words, in her English accent, from the Point Atkinson Lighthouse station, which also really exists, on a point of land in West Vancouver. It was here in 1871 that the federal government built a light to help coax British Columbia into Canada. The station she and her keeper husband, Donald, moved into in 1980 had been rebuilt sixty-eight years earlier on the foundation of the first light. She lives there still, even though the station turned automated in 1996 and her husband—who worked in tandem with another man as the light's last keepers—died five years later.

It's her home, but it's also a museum. Someday that's what every lighthouse in this country will be. At that point, a dramatic human narrative will have run its course. Death brought the first light stations to this land: along the coast of British Columbia, where the mouth of Juan de Fuca is nicknamed the "graveyard of the Pacific" because of the large numbers of shipwrecks there in the days before light stations were built.

But also on the east coast, where wrecks led to the construction of a lighthouse at the summit of Gull Island, off Newfoundland's Bay de Verde Peninsula after a sealer discovered the bodies of fourteen passengers and the crew from the Welsh brigantine *Queen of Swansea* in 1868. Lighthouses, in time, stood on Sable Island, a spit of land known as the "graveyard of the Atlantic," where since 1583 there have been some 350 recorded shipwrecks. They blinked on both ends of St. Paul Island, north of Cape Breton, where each spring fishermen from the mainland would find the frozen bodies of shipwrecked seamen huddled in crude shelters, waiting for help that never came.

The waters around Seal Island, off the southwest tip of Nova Scotia, were particularly treacherous. Before anyone lived on the island, shipwrecked mariners who reached its shores routinely died of starvation and exposure during the harsh winters. By the early years of the nineteenth century, a grim tradition had evolved: every spring preachers and residents from the mainland villages of Yarmouth and Barrington would get in boats and make their way to the island to find and bury the winter's dead. One year twenty-one people had to be buried in shallow graves in a single day.

In 1823, two families, the Hichens and the Crowells, settled on the island in the hope of assisting the unfortunate souls cast ashore during the winter storms. In time, Richard Hichens, who himself had been shipwrecked on Cape Sable, married Mary Crowell, who had heard first-hand many stories of the deaths on Seal Island from her father, a Barrington preacher. On the night of November 28, 1831, the island's fixed light was lit for the first time. That same evening a daughter was born to Richard and Mary, thus beginning a family light-keeping tradition that would last more than a century on Seal Island.

By the turn of the nineteenth century, Canada had more than eight hundred manned lighthouses. They stood on lonely islands and in the harbours of burgeoning metropolises. A few even winked in the Prairie province of Manitoba. In the country with the longest coastline in the world, the keepers kept the light on in the dark. They guided the ships and sailors home. From the beginning, they were the heroic men and women who climbed into boats in weather capable of sending schooners and brigantines to the bottom, to come to the aid of the shipwrecked.

Yet as I write these words, there are precisely fifty-one manned lighthouses in Canada: twenty-seven in British Columbia, twenty-three in Newfoundland and Labrador and one in New Brunswick. What the heck happened? Technology, mostly. New equipment meant it was no longer necessary to have a human on-site to operate lights and activate foghorns. Radar, radio beacons, satellite-based global positioning systems and advances in communications made navigation more reliable and safer for anyone with a boat that had the technology. Between 1970 and 1996, 264 lighthouses—including every one in Nova Scotia, Quebec, Prince Edward Island and Ontario—were automated. Keepers' houses were razed. Lighthouses were destroyed, replaced by utilitarian skeleton-tower lights. Many of the buildings that remained standing were abandoned and left to vandals. Individuals and entire communities stepped forward to save the historic stations. But red tape made it hard to do much.

That was just the way the universe seemed to be going: by then a few countries with remote and expansive coastlines, like

Chile and Brazil, still had staffed lights. A few technicians in charge of operating and maintaining navigational aids could be found in lighthouses in Portugal and Denmark. But Australia had de-staffed its stations. Every lighthouse in the United States was by then automated and only one, Boston Light, still had a government-paid keeper.

Only the loudness of the public outcry saved the last of the keepers in British Columbia and Newfoundland and Labrador. The government ran into such resistance that it abandoned a 1998 plan to remove the light keepers in those provinces. A year later it tabled, then put on hold, another bill designed to do the same thing. Before long the government was back with its Heritage Lighthouse Protection Act, under which it declared 487 active and 488 inactive lighthouses "surplus" to Canada's requirements. The fifty staffed light stations in British Columbia and Newfoundland and Labrador were, for the moment, safe. In 2010, according to a Senate report, British Columbia's lights employed thirty-seven full-time staff.

Which, I guess, is where this book began.

~

LIGHT keepers, there can be little doubt, will someday soon take their place alongside voyageurs and trappers, match-makers and milliners. At some point, they will invariably join buffalo hunters, whalers and buggy whip makers. In time, their names will stand on a roll that includes seamstresses and steeplejacks, butchers and bootblacks, cobblers and clock-makers, gandy dancers and gravediggers. Their day is surely coming, just as it is for nuns, long-haul truckers, general-store owners and telephone linemen. The die is cast. It is written in stone. The fat lady has sung. Technological change, anyone can see, is part of it. Other cruel forces are also at work here. The dogged pursuit of "efficiencies." But also a global marketplace that doesn't just mean you can sell your goods or services to Mumbai; it means those smart, fast, hungry folks in Shanghai can sell their stuff in Moose Jaw or Little Heart's Ease. The way things stand, that's not really a fair fight.

And so there goes the old world, the world most of us are used to. The numbers don't lie: in 1871 when Canada was a new country, just 19 percent of us lived in cities. Today 81 percent of us make our homes where it's possible to get a Starbucks latte or see Quentin Tarantino gore on the big screen. That's out of necessity as well as choice. Of the nearly seventeen million people working in this country in 2006, the time of the last census, nearly one-third worked in sales and service occupations, while another three million were in business, finance and administration jobs. In other words, they did city work.

The Statistics Canada folk, on the other hand, found just 3,000 boat builders, 2,000 shoe repairers and 6,000 jewellers and watch repairers. Some 21,000 men and women operated printing presses. Another 31,000 made fine furniture. But our waterfronts employed just 6,000 longshoremen. In this big country, there were only 4,000 land surveyors and 7,000 people who made maps. Some of the juxtapositions were disheartening: there were 12,000 librarians, compared with 20,000 Canadians working in casinos. More people described themselves as "image consultants" than funeral directors and embalmers. The total number of auditors, accountants and investment professionals—315,000—was more than all the carpenters, electricians, cabinetmakers, roofers and glaziers in this country put together.

What about the people we talked about in this book? Public relations and communications practitioners outnumbered writers and journalists. There were 870 blacksmiths in Canada in 2006, a category that also included die setters. About 10,000 men and a few women operated our trains. There were 200,000 farmers. These people may not necessarily disappear tomorrow. But my travels didn't make me think that their offspring could dream, with any assurance, of following in the family business, be it operating the projector at a drive-in movie, selling records or delivering milk.

If I live long enough, one day in the not-distant future I'll sit a grandchild or two on my knee and tell them all about those folks. Like one of those ancient coots going on about the good ole days, I'll enlighten them about other things too: about friends, family and a life that, to one kid in one small city at the far end of the continent, seemed golden. If I really get going, I'll even tell them about what it was like in 1967, when the land seemed to vibrate with possibility and everything we wanted—even if we didn't know quite what that was—was out there shimmering on the horizon.

I'll slap my thigh like Walter Brennan. Then I'll tell them how it was to mosey around in the neighbourhood where I now write these words. It's smaller than it seemed then. It always is when some codger goes back to visit the stomping ground of youth. Back then, after all, you were just a kid who was close to the ground, so everything seemed huge. The universe seemed bigger because days stretched longer before instant messaging and *Call of Duty*.

There was space back in the time of fountain pens, pond hockey and Saturday matinees. The possibilities were infinite when you were left to your own designs so long as you returned intact for supper, as the evening meal was known in many of our households in those olden times.

Parents, at least in this neighbourhood, didn't worry about bad stuff happening because nothing bad ever really happened to anybody. So we were free, like gap-toothed, snot-nosed Odysseuses, to wander. Near on half a century later I walk these streets still, hoping for a glimpse of a kid who was often seen in these parts: Adidas-shod, Levi's-clad, pockets bulging with pennies, lint, Bob Pulford hockey cards, a half-eaten bag of Planters peanuts. He was, I know for a fact, often running. It was not a graceful act. But no one was there to see it. He was just a boy. This was just a street. Back in the innocent days.

ACKNOWLEDGEMENTS

The most obvious debts of thanks for this book are to the subjects themselves who so generously gave me unfettered access to their lives.

An immense thanks goes out to Paul McNeil, who used his vast community newspaper web to help me throughout the course of this book. I'm also deeply indebted to renaissance man Chris Mills—writer, broadcaster, lighthouse keeper and lover of black rum—for his knowledge of all things related to coastal lights. Endlessly creative blacksmith John Little, as well was a huge help.

My wise agent Dean Cooke made this book happen. At Doubleday Canada, Tim Rostron and freelance copyeditor Beverley Sotolov took my unhewn lumber and fashioned it into something; designer Five Seventeen made it look good; Susan Burns oversaw the creation.

A big shout out to my children, Belle and Sam, for their encouragement and keeping me grounded in the here-and-now. The biggest thanks, as always, to Lisa Napier for, well, everything.

NOTES

PROLOGUE

Pierre Berton's line about 1967 in Canada is from his book, *1967: The Last Good Year*, Doubleday Canada, 1997.

The information about the jobs of yesteryear came from the 1911 Census of Canada p. 14-29.

The forecasts about the expected declines in traditional jobs came from Frank Feather, *Canada's Best Career Guide 2000*, Warwick Books, 1999

Malcolm Gladwell's thoughts on satisfying work come from his book *Outliers: The Story of Success*, Little, Brown & Company, 2008, p. 149-151

Daniel Gilbert's thoughts come from his article "Times to Remember, Times to Forget," *The New York Times*, Dec. 30, 2009

CHAPTER ONE: ACROSS THIS LAND

The information about the relationship between the formation of Canada and railways comes from *The Canadian Encyclopedia: Canada Since Confederation* along with *National Policy and the CPR—Canadian History Portal*.

The information about the formation of Via Rail comes from various sources.

The specs for the Canadian come from Via Rail.

The list of railway lingo comes from Jordan McCallum and other sources.

The figures on railways comes from the Central Intelligence Agency 2011 http://www.mapsofworld.com/world-top-ten/longest-rail-network.html

The information on how the rail system works in Canada comes from Jordan McCallum and Craig Stead.

The information on railway accidents comes from the Transportation Safety Board of Canada's 1999 rail stats and an assortment of other sources.

CHAPTER TWO: HOLY SWEET MOTHER

The information about the gender makeup of Canadian veterinary colleges comes from the "Canadian Colleges of Veterinary Medicine" entry in the *Canadian Encyclopedia*.

CHAPTER THREE: THE MILKMAN COMETH

The section on the Divco truck comes from Robert R. Ebert and John S. Rienzo Jr., Divco, *A History of the Truck and Company*, Antique Power Inc. Yellow Springs, Ohio, 1997, p. iii

Some of the information about the historical duties of the milkman comes from the Palo Alto History.com, a website devoted to the history of Palo Alto, California.

I interviewed Les Bagley, director of the Divco Club of America via email.

The reasons for the decline in milk consumption come from Wendi Hiebert's food blog FoodWise.

The information on declining milk delivery comes via an email exchange with the Canadian Dairy Commission.

The information on Farmers Dairy comes from a number of sources including Grant Gerke, Farmers Dairy's form/fill/seal system creates new landscape, *Packaging Digest 2003* and author's interview with Catherine Ludovice, marketing director Farmers Dairy.

The figure about urban populations in Canada comes from Statistics Canada. http://www.statcan.gc.ca/pub/11-008-x/2007004/ 10313-eng.htm

The information on the negative impacts of working at night comes from Brandon Keim, "Nightshift makes Metabolism Go Haywire," *Wired Science*, March 2, 2009; Navdeep Kaur Marwah, "Women Working the Night Shift Inch Closer to Breast Cancer," *MSN, Midday*, March 4, 2009; "Working the Night Shift May be Hazardous to Your Health," *Health News*, Sept. 29, 2009 and Kenneth Macdonald, "Night Shifts Spark Cancer Pay-Out," *BBC*, March 15, 2009.

CHAPTER FOUR: WATERING HOLE FOR DREAMERS

The information on the history of Sam the Record Man comes from http://news.library.ryerson.ca/musiconyonge/"a-historical-corner/

The information on the big department stores in Canada comes from a variety of sources but mainly The Department Store Museum website http://departmentstoremuseum.blogspot.ca which includes the floor plan for the Toronto Simpson's.

The information about the recording industry came from http://blogs.wsj.com/economics/2011/03/28/top-10-dying-industries/

The Michael Chabon line comes from his book *Telegraph Avenue*, HarperCollins Publishers Ltd., 2012, p.7

CHAPTER FIVE: EVERY JESELLY ONE OF THEM

The information about the 2003 election comes from "PEI Votes—and Votes and Votes," John DeMont, *Macleans* magazine, Oct. 13, 2003 and http://results.elections.on.ca/results/2003_results/stat_sum_totals.jsp.

The number of Atlantic Journalism Awards won by Prince Edward Island media outlets comes from the Atlantic Journalism Awards.

The notion of the ephemeral nature of Google searches was explored in depth by Robert D. Kaplan in "Cultivating Loneliness," *The Columbia Journalism Review,* January/February 2006.

The information for the Montague history section comes from the Town of Montague's website.

The portrait of Jim MacNeill came from "The Common Touch: a colorful publisher stirs the pot in PEI," John DeMont, *Macleans,* May 9, 1994, interviews with his son Paul and MacNeill's friend, the singer and entrepreneur Denis Ryan as well as David Cadogan's May 21, 1998 eulogy for MacNeill.

The sampling of stories and advertisements in the *Eastern Graphic* came from the paper during July 29 and Aug. 12, 2010.

The rural depopulation information comes from Census Snapshot of Canada – Urbanization, Statistics Canada, 222.statcan.gc.ca

CHAPTER SIX: IRON MAN

Information about the history of blacksmithing comes from The History of Blacksmithing, the National Blacksmiths and Welders Association

The Kane & Son website is https://www.blacksmithsdepot.com.

The quote from Richard Sennet, is from his book *The Craftsman,* Yale University Press, 2008, p. 9

The figures on jobs in Quebec are from the 1911 Census of Canada.

The information on blacksmithing in Quebec comes from J.C. Dupont's *Canadian Encyclopedia* entry on the Blacksmith's Trade in the Province of Quebec.

The information on Lloyd Johnston comes from http://www.waybacktimes.com/blacksmith83.html as well as a catalogue entry about his work: http://www.warehamforge.ca/gravegoods/catalog/johnson.html

The geographical information about the Great Plains comes from the *Great Plains Encyclopedia*. http://plainshumanities.unl.edu/encyclopedia/

The person per acre ratio for the Special Areas comes from the history section of the Special Areas Board's website http://specialareas.ab.ca/profile/history

The quote about the history of Hanna, Alberta comes from the history section on the town's website http://www.hanna.ca/Visitors/History.aspx

The Canadian governments recruitment efforts to settle the west come from the Canadian Museum of Civilization's exhibit: "The Last Best West: Advertising for Immigrants to Western Canada, 1870-1930." http://www.civilization.ca/cmc/exhibitions/hist/advertis/ads6-01e.shtml. As well as the *Canadian Encyclopedia*'s entry on "Ranching History." http://www.thecanadianencyclopedia.com/articles/ranching-history and Curtis McManus's history master's thesis at the University of Saskatchewan, *Happyland: the Agricultural crisis in Saskatchewan's Drybelt, 1917-27.*

The estimate for the numbers of Americans who immigrated to the Canadian west come from Karel Denis Bicha, Proceedings of the American Philosophical Society, Vol. 109, No. 6 (Dec. 10, 1965), p. 398-440.

The Palliser quote comes from Exploration-British North America—the journals, detailed reports, and observations relative to the exploration, by Captain Palliser, of that portion of British North America, which, in latitude, lies between the British boundary line and the height of land or watershed of the northern or frozen ocean respectively, and in longitude, between the western shore of Lake Superior and the Pacific Ocean during the years 1857, 1858, 1859, and 1860, John Palliser, p. 4

G.A. French's quotes come from David Jones, "We'll all be buried Down Here: the Prairie Dryland Disaster, 1917-1926," published by the Historical Society of Alberta, Calgary, Alta, 1986, p. 2.

Jones' description of the conditions during that period comes from David Jones, *Empire of Dust: Settling and Abandoning the Prairie Dry Belt*, University of Calgary Press, 2002-09-01, p. 44.

The overwrought journalistic description of Southern Alberta comes from the same book by Jones, p. 33

The increase in Alberta's population in the 1920s comes from the website Forgotten Alberta http://forgottenalberta.com/about/

The fact that wheat was the main crop on most of the Alberta farms during this period comes from Gregory Marchildon, "Institutional Adaptation to Drought and the Special Areas of Alberta, 1909-1939," p. 9 http://www.parc.ca/mcri/pdfs/papers/iacc038.pdf.

The statistics about cattle farming come from Statistics Canada 's 2011 Farm and farm operator data. http://www29.statcan.gc.ca/ceag-web/eng/community-agriculture-profile-profil-agricole.action?geoId=480000000&selectedVarIds=242

The information about Jack Nestor comes from Marj Venot and from Jack Nester's obituary in the *Hanna Herald*, May, 2010

CHAPTER EIGHT: LIFE OF A SALESMAN

History of Shawville comes from the town's website http://town.shawville.qc.ca/web

The breakdown of Shawville's population comes from the 2001 Census of Canada.

The story about the language inspector comes from Dave Rogers, "Where Have the Angry Anglos Gone," *Ottawa Citizen*, July 24, 2010

The W. Francis Gates rules come from his book *Tips for the Traveling Salesman*, B.C. Forbes Publishing Co. 120 Fifth Ave., New York City, 1929. The anecdote about American sales firms handing out spiels for their agents to use comes from p. 5 in that book.

The Epstein story comes from John DeMont, *Coal Black Heart: The Story of Coal and the Lives it Ruled*, Doubleday Canada, 2009, p. 163

The information about the Newfoundland peddlers comes from Jenny Higgins Newfoundland and Labrador Heritage Web site.

The information for the section on Syrian peddlers in the West, including the quote from Gilbert Johnson comes via Andrea W. Lorenz, "Canada's Pioneer Mosque," *Saudi Aramco World*, vol. 49, no. 4. The history of peddlers in the rest of Canada comes from: Andrew Armitage, "Peddlers Once a Common Sight," *The Sun Times* (Owen Sound), April 24, 2009 and Benita Baker, "Rag and Bone Men," *The Beaver*, December, 2004 which was also the source of the *Macleans* magazine quote about peddlers and the quote from Allan Grossman's autobiography.

The information from Terry Carruthers, chief executive officer of the North West Commercial Traveller's Association of Canada came from a telephone interview with the author.

I based my estimate for the number of sales call Steve has made during his career on a conservative six sales calls a day for 250 days a year over 38 years. It could just as easily be twice that number.

CHAPTER NINE: SHOWTIME

The early days of drive-in movies comes from various sources.

The summary about the end of the good times for drive-ins comes from *Shining Stars: Canada's Drive-in Movie Theatres*, a 2004 documentary by KarowPrime Films. Some of the information about how drive-ins used to work comes from the same film.

The drive-in job figures come from "Movie Theatres and Drive-Ins," Statistics Canada, June 28, 2005. I based my estimate on drive-in movies in Canada by taking driveinmovie.com's figure of a peak of 4,000 drive-in screens in North America and then dividing that by 10. The figure on annual drive-in customers in Canada comes from "Drive-in movies attract new generation," CBCNews.ca July 14, 2006.

Carl Weese's commentary is from "The American Drive-in Movie Theater," a 2007 show at the Washington Art Association, Washington, Connecticut. I first read of him in Shane Dixon Kavanaugh, "Showcase: Dark Screens, Bright Memories," *The New York Times*, Jan. 15, 2010.

The description of life in a lighthouse comes from sources within
the light-keeping community who, for obvious reasons, wish to
remain anonymous.

The world history of lighthouses comes from a variety of sources.

The Louisbourg lighthouse information comes from a variety of
entries on the Louisbourg Lighthouse Society websight http://
fortress.cbu.ca/LouisbourgLighthouseSociety/.

The information about the Bull Island, Nfld. lighthouse came from
Lighthouse Digest http://www.lighthousedigest.com/Digest/
StoryPage.cfm?StoryKey=1988.

The information about the St. Paul Island lighthouse came from
http://www.nslps.com/light-detail.aspx?ID=272&M=IP&N=2.

The figure for the number of lighthouses in Canada at the turn of the
19th century comes from author's interview with Chris Mills.

The author interviewed Elaine Graham via telephone.

For information on the recent saga of lighthouses in Canada I
leaned heavily upon *Seeing The Light: Report on Staffed Lighthouses
in Newfoundland Labrador and British Columbia*, "Report of the
Standing Senate Committee on Fisheries and Oceans," Bill
Rompkey, Chair December 2010 and "Implementation of the
Heritage Lighthouse Protection Act," Report of the Standing
Senate Committee on Fisheries and Oceans, Bill Rompkey
Chair, March 2011

The job numbers in this chapter came from the 2006 Census of
Canada.